"This is a beautiful and hone:
loss and grief. Dai's catharti
and written prayers paints a I
a grieving son who finds com
Father."

"This is a wonderful, brave, honest and incredibly helpful book. For one so young, Dai has experienced both grief and burnout. That he has navigated both of these experiences so well is an amazing testament to Dai, but even more so are the lessons he has learned through it all. With his story and poetry he explains the pain and loss but also gives hope for a way through both. I encourage you to read it – it will inspire, challenge and, hopefully, help you avoid burnout. But above all, the prose and poems will be your 'friend' when you face loss and the pain of grief."

"Dai's words are both beautifully and brutally honest about how grief ravages the heart. Some books tell you how to cope with grief. This book helps guide you home."

"Dai's writing is a rare gift to us all. He has the creative soul of a poet combined with the straightforward honesty of a friend. You'll feel like you know him, as you share this personal but powerfully uplifting book. These carefully crafted pages and prayers are sure to be a blessing to us all as we all navigate the realities of life and death together."

"Dai is a born writer and a brilliant communicator. Not many can cut to the nub of an issue with warmth, humour and accessibility – especially a Big Subject like grief. Dai has just the right amount of playfulness in his bones to connect with people but make them think, properly think. He's got talent in spades and thankfully he's shovelled those spades into this book."

Paul Kerensa, Comedian and Writer (*Miranda*, *Top Gear*, *TFI Friday*, *Not Going Out*)

"Prayers, Texts and Tears *allows us to see into not just Dai's heart... but his soul. Honest, at times funny, heartbreaking... and perhaps, above all... real."*

Rob Parsons, OBE

"Dai and I were mentored by the same guy. He modelled to us a wonderfully Welsh way of ministry: confession, creativity and comedy. These three elements can be woven together to create a bespoke pastoral care. In this little book with a big heart, Dai employs his masterly gifts in these three areas. Abounding in real and raw honesty, furnished with beautiful and balm-like poetry, and laced with well-timed humorous whit, this book is a precious gift that points us to the ultimate Anchor in our seas of grief."

Jonathan Thomas, Minister, Cornerstone Evangelical Church, Abergavenny

PRAYERS TEXTS + TEARS

A CREATIVE RESPONSE TO GRIEF

DAI WOOLRIDGE

MONARCH
BOOKS

Oxford, UK, and Grand Rapids, USA

Published by Monarch Books (an imprint of Lion Hudson plc)
Wilkinson House, Jordan Hill Road, Oxford OX2 8DR, England
Email: monarch@lionhudson.com www.lionhudson.com/monarch
and by Elevation (an imprint of the Memralife Group)
Memralife Group, 14 Horsted Square, Uckfield, East Sussex TN22 1QG
Tel: +44 (0)1825 746530; Fax +44 (0)1825 748899;
www.elevationmusic.com

ISBN 978 0 85721 777 6
e-ISBN 978 0 85721 778 3

First edition 2017

Acknowledgments
Unless otherwise mentioned, Scripture quotations taken from are from
The Holy Bible, English Standard Version® (ESV®) copyright © 2001 by
Crossway, a publishing ministry of Good News Publishers. All rights reserved.
Scripture quotations marked marked NIV taken from the Holy Bible, New
International Version Anglicised. Copyright © 1979, 1984, 2011 Biblica,
formerly International Bible Society. Used by permission of Hodder &
Stoughton Ltd, an Hachette UK company. All rights reserved. "NIV" is a
registered trademark of Biblica. UK trademark number 1448790.

A catalogue record for this book is available from the British Library

Printed and bound in the UK, January 2017, LH26

For Dad

Father, friend, and forever missed

By Jessica Woolridge

CONTENTS

ACKNOWLEDGMENTS

There are many who are worthy of a thank you, but these are my highlights...

A big thanks to the lovely Becki Bradshaw – you've empowered and gently guided me on this journey. You believed in me and this book when it was nothing more than a conviction in my gut and a bucket of emotions in my heart.

Thanks to Drew, Jenny, Roger and the team at Lion Hudson for your editing and layout skills.

Thank you Lois – what a privilege to have you work your visual magic on this book. Thanks for bringing my words to life.

Thank you Bob – your friendship, fun, guidance, and creativity mean so much. Thanks for bribing Becki to come and see me in action. If this book is my baby, you're the matchmaker who put me and Lion Hudson together. (I just made that weird didn't I?)

Thank you to those who offered up writing seat places.

To the guys at Nicholaston House for the epic views, to Phil and Marianne for giving space for my book to breathe.

Thank you to JT, Sammy, Wyn, Emz, and the AEC family for how you have served us as a family over the years, and for helping me give my old man a great send off.

Thank you to the SOW and Going Public family; to Jesslyn, Jordyn, Hannah, Cath, and Madoc for how you stepped in last minute with the Coffee Shop Tour.

Thank you Pope Francis of Glenwood, Norman Wisdom Adams, Rob Burns and the whole Glenwood family for your prayers, guidance and support.

Thank you to the lounge family (past and present) for your love and prayers. Thanks to the boys for the breakies, beers, pool, and rugby jeering.

Thank you most epic friends. Thank you Steve and Katie, Hedd and Jess, Matt and Amz.

Thank you Ads and Rach for your amazing friendship. For the love and laughs which brought lightness in the dark times, for being such a support throughout my grief journey.

Thank you Marian and Chris for your support in the toughest four days of my life yet.

Thank you Evans family. Als for your creative counsel. Walt and Gar for all the generosity and love you have shown me. I can honestly say you're the best in-laws I've ever had (and I really do mean that).

Thank you Jess – so gifted. Proud of all you are and all you're becoming

Thank you Dylan – for being the amazing brother you are who never ceases to put a smile on my face.

Thank you Mam – for everything. For how you looked after us and how you continue to pour out your loving affection on us, even when it costs you yourself. Thank you for being such a rock in those final days. You're a blessing and the greatest "Mam" I could've hoped for.

Thank you to my most beautiful inside and out wife. My bestie for the restie. My Bobs. Thank you for loving me when I'm broken and semi-whole. For holding my hand through every step of this hilly, off-road grief journey. The tough bits and the teary bits. You're my everything and I'm so privileged to be on the receiving end of your love. Love you always,and forever yours. Dafs (a.k.a. Dale) x

And lastly, thank you to my risen Saviour, my loving Father and the great Comforter. To be known by you, makes life worth living. I couldn't have come this far, without You. You are my All.

FOREWORD by Bob Hartman

In his book, *Telling the Truth*, the novelist and theologian Frederick Buechner says that before we have the right to tell anyone the "good news", we must first demonstrate to them that we understand the reality of the "bad news".

This came home to me in a powerful way a few years ago, when I wrote and performed a retelling of the story of the widow of Nain's son.

As part of that retelling, I tried to imagine how the widow might have felt, and suggested that she was not only devastated by her son's death, but also angry. Angry at God, for letting him die. And angry, even, with her neighbours and friends who had gathered to support her at her son's funeral. Angry, because they still had sons and husbands of their own, to be there with them.

Following the performance, a woman came up to me, tears in her eyes, to say thank you. She had suffered a devastating loss as well, and her thanks was not so much for the part of the story where the boy came back to life, but for the part where the mother expressed her anger. She had felt the same anger, she said, but she had never heard anyone admit that. And so she found it comforting.

In that situation, the "good news" not only followed the "bad news", it actually arose from it, the two inseparably joined together.

I think that's the case with Dai's book. His willingness to invite us into his grief, and to do so in such an honest fashion, provides a context where we can not only see grief at work, but also discover with him the ways in which hope arises from it.

It is his vulnerability, laid bare before us, that allows us to be vulnerable with him. And having experienced that – the truth of it, and the pain – we are then ready to journey with him as he finds his way through it. There is nothing cliched, nothing pat, and no hint of the ten-easy-steps-for-overcoming-grief approach that plagues so many books. It is the "good news" and "the bad news" all mashed uncomfortably together, as Buechner recognised, and as experience affirms, particularly in those times where life seems to want to crush us.

It helps, of course, that Dai has a wonderful way with words. He demonstrates that through his lovely and accessible conversational style. It really is like sitting down and having a chat with him at your local coffee shop (or The Guns at Avoncliffe, mate!). But there is also his poetry, the medium for which he is better known. They complement each other and give us two equally compelling windows into his grief.

A shout out to his wife Cath, as well, who helps us to see Dai's pain through her eyes. In fact, it is the presence of family that makes this book work so well. We really do feel like we know Dai's family, particularly his dad, who is at the heart of it all. And even though, at times, it all seems a bit mixed up and messed up and broken up – much like grief itself – it is also gloriously filled up with the loving memories and shared moments that make up every set of relationships.

It is, as Buechner suggests, "good news" and "bad news", all rolled into one. And therefore the place from which God speaks His news. Of comfort. And healing. And hope.

Messy Grief...

Grief isn't pretty.
It's not clean-cut, neat and tidy faith.
It's not prim and proper.

Grief isn't nice and fluffy
It's not cute kittens and rainbows

Grief isn't holier than thou.
It's not fun central or party time
And it doesn't involve lots of selfies.
It's gritty.
At times it's flat-out ugly so keep your selfie sticks to
    yourself.

Grief is more than a cliché
It's not a boat in a storm with sunshine in the distance
It's not a silhouette with drooped shoulders or
A guy on a bed with his head in his hands.

Grief's not just some article you read about
And you don't tackle it with superficial pat answers.

Grief's not a one-time deal
It's a time and time again that gets easier over time deal
Grief doesn't cope well with being swept under the rug
And sometimes it shows up unannounced

Grief's not something you can file or shred.
It's not something you can recycle down a yard, centre,
or bottle bank.

You can't empty it from your recycling bin
Or take it back within 14 days in exchange for store
credit.

Grief is not just something for the non-churchy types
Grief transcends class, haircut, skin tone, religion, and
pay package.

Grief is inappropriate
Grief is socially awkward
Grief is uncomfortable
Grief is edgy
Grief is raw, real, and probably something else
beginning with "r"
It's messy.
You may already know it.
But please, allow me to introduce you to
Messy Grief.

Grief's mine, hands off...

It's important to stress I don't own the rights to grief. I'm not the guy who strolls in late to a party, throws the DJ off his decks, and lets rip with his own playlist.

Many people have suffered this heartache. There's also been good stuff written on this subject matter; for me *A Grief Observed* by C. S. Lewis is an absolute must-read – it's less of a book and more of a window into his own hurting.

So why's yours truly taking a stab at this issue?

Well, for starters I've been going through it since I was twenty-eight.

Writing this book has taken me a few more steps down the grief journey and a few more scars have faded along the way but, like I said, though grief gets easier it's not a one-time deal.

Why am I writing this book? I guess you could call it a calling.

In the Brad Pitt of my grief, the thought of writing anything to do with God, let alone penning the pit of grief itself, would send me into a panic.

Yet as I sat in the doctor's surgery waiting room (finally accepting my need for help), I had a conviction that one day there was going to be a book. It was the first time I really understood the life-sapping, hope-thieving nature of grief.

"So this is how it feels."

Then I thought about all those who may be going through something similar. People who were struggling to get by on any given day. How do they cope? Do they know they're not alone?

In this book, I wanted as much as possible to bare my soul. To prise it open and show you what's inside: the faith bits, the gritty bits, and the… tough bits.

Just as you've opened up this book (or downloaded and swiped… or even synced and played), so I wanted to open myself up to you, to download bits of myself, sync my soul, and play to you bits of my prayer, faith, and life and what that looked like during my toughest time yet.

One bind... two edges

My hope is that this will be one book with two covers.

One cover...

To give a voice to so many people who feel like they're on mute in their suffering.

To give people room to revisit the unopened hurts and gently invite those people to un-pause their grief.

I want to help the grief strugglers find faith nuggets, healing moments and peace places as I share my struggles, faith nuggets and healing moments; along with the places where peace has penetrated the anguish.

The other cover...

I wanted this to be a book for those who have never really grieved.

For those trying to connect with grief carriers…

For the friends, family, co-workers, and partners…

It'll be worth sharing my story if it somehow helps you understand grief just that little bit more.

Some three and a half years on, I offer you my collection of scribbles and inner monologues, which have been jotted down and typed up over the last nine months. I offer them humbly, with some psalm prayers and my hunch on what I believe God would be saying back. You can use these as stand-alone poems if you want, though I'm not going to go through another bout of grief if you don't... it's totally up to you! You'll find some stuff you can check out on YouTube too. I've even slipped in a "Dai Dictionary" at the end of each chapter in case you don't have a *badger's stethoscope** what I'm on about.

My hope is that this book will help put into words what is so hard to express. My prayer is that you will find God to be the ultimate Carrier of grief carriers.

Finally, this book is a tribute to the man that it's about.

An amazing man.

A funny man.

A take no messing but full on love giving man.

A do anything for anyone man.

A see the best in everyone man.

A constantly in pain but sucked it up and got on with it man.

A lover of loud rock music man.

A talking storyteller man.

A bike enthusiast man.

A denim jacket with lots of badges man.

A hater of anything with garlic in it man.

A Jim Carrey impressions man.

DAI DICTIONARY

A man who was sometimes misunderstood.

Dad, I love you and miss you every day.

"Ger* who's not all there"...

This book's for you pal.

Dave*

Badger's stethoscope – "I don't know what this is either!?"

Ger – affectionate nickname for the old man, Dad. "Ger" was often followed by "ald".

Just a heads-up – Dai is Welsh for Dave, hence the sign-off here.

THE SITUATION
THAT'S AROUND
ME, THIS PAIN IT
ASTOUNDS ME,
THE NUMBNESS IT
SURROUNDS ME

I'M HERE I'M NEAR
I'M ONLINE
CLOSE BY

Chapter

1

WORLD-CRUSHING

It was Monday morning in my church. And just as every Monday morning, the day started with a staff meeting. Church leaders, youth workers, administrators, and interns all gathered in a semicircle to reflect on the previous week and pray for the next. It was always a laugh – there'd be a bit of a buzz as people caught up on the week and others darted to the kitchen to whip up a cuppa before the meeting started.

And then to the meeting – in the midst of quick quips and slurps of tea there'd be a reflective "God bit" from that day, and then we'd go around the room with our prayer requests. I'd like to say I remember the God bit, but I don't.

What I do remember though was a colleague's moving prayer request for his friend who had cancer. The details are a little hazy but this friend was a missionary in Scotland, though originally from the States, and her efforts to get home were proving impossible because of the C word – cancer. I remember Mark filling up with tears as he poured his heart out about his friend's dire situation, yet at the same time remembering her faithful service to the Lord. (I'm welling up now just recalling it.) We prayed, the meeting finished, and I offered my condolences to Mark afterwards.

The rest of the morning was pretty routine, reading through a sketch I had written with another colleague, Hannah. During pen-scribbled note-taking and "From the top?" moments were some missed calls from a number I didn't recognize. I decided to press on as we were getting into a bit of a rhythm (for a poet, rhythm's important). After the practice I returned to my desk and to-do list, and then remembered the missed calls.

I pick up my phone to a voicemail from the hospital.

"Mr Woolridge, we've been trying to reach you concerning your father. Please call us back as soon as you get this message," says a flat-toned nurse's voice.

I freeze as an avalanche of thoughts pick up pace and start to overwhelm me.

OK, let me back up a little. That same morning I had also asked for prayer for my dad. You see, he was in hospital after being in a bit of a bad way the week before. He was admitted on the Wednesday and I had got down to see him on the Friday. He had lost weight, a lot of weight. With a military background, Dad had always been of a lean build and because of an eating disorder, he frequently took prescribed protein shakes just to keep his weight on. But this was different; a 5 ft 11 man weighing in at a mere six stone something was still a shock. When we had seen him on the Friday he was a little dazed, but a helpful nutritionist had had a calming effect on all of us as she encouraged Dad to get "tubed up" with essential nutrients. We didn't know what was wrong then, but staring us in the face was the fact that the fragile frame he now possessed was not going to hack it.

Nutrients + hydration = strength

(A simpler equation than 2 + 2.)

On Saturday I had checked in with the hospital and received some good news. Dad had picked up. Now hydrated, he was walking round the ward – he had even had a shave (again, his military background – a presentable appearance is important, even when you're rocking a hospital gown!).

With that news, peace returned to me and I was thankful. However, to paraphrase my dad, I think I was "lulled into a false sense of nutrient security". You see, hydration can only do so much.

Skip forward two days and we're back to Monday, post read-through, post hospital voicemail.

I call to find out that Dad has taken a turn for the worse and they suggest I come down as soon as I can. This wasn't part of the plan. I'd already made arrangements to visit Dad after work – but this wasn't about fitting into my schedule, it was more of a "drop everything, handbrake down, and shift down the M4 as fast as the speed limit permits" plan, if not a little quicker.

Sarah, my office buddy, picks up the gist of the conversation and, sensing the turmoil seeping through my pores, just tells me to be safe as I drive.

I pick up my wife Cath and my sister Jess. We fuel up on petrol and sandwiches, and an hour and a bit later we're watching Dad being carted off for a scan. He's alert, but he doesn't look good.

Mam*, Auntie Marian, and my brother Dylan meet us there.

"Where's David?" asks a female doctor.

"That's me," I say, as I'm fighting off that frightened feeling.

The doctor, forty-something and 5 ft nothing, seems approachable yet professional. As the next of kin she calls me in to her office, a small room just a catheter's throw away from Dad's bed. She barely starts speaking before the rest of the family come in too, anxious to know the score.

There's a slight pause.

"It's not good news I'm afraid. Your father's got pancreatic cancer. It's spread and unfortunately there's nothing we can do. I'm sorry."

I pause. I don't know for how long; in these moments time seems to slow down. Like in that final scene of *The Matrix** where Neo turns from Chuck Bartowski* into Chuck Norris* (or vice versa depending what season of "Chuck" you're on). Like that, but less cool and more gut-wrenching.

With a stress-induced stammer I ask about the timescale:

"Uh… Is, is it days, wuh-weeks, mu-mu-months?"

She says it's probably a matter of days.

I can't remember what exactly happened next but I do remember a sudden clarity that anything else that had been contending for my thoughts before this moment paled into insignificance.

The doctor asks what would be best, to tell Dad or not.

"He'll want to know," we say.

"Would you prefer I tell him the news or would you like to?"

Like is a funny word. I *like* brownies, I *like* watching Blu-ray films with big explosions, or browsing BBC Sport for the latest rugby articles. This is not going to make the list of things that I "like". The doctor told Dad. I wasn't there when he did. But he took it well, as well as you could take news like that. He asked how long he had, and was determined to make it three weeks, to 28 February. His fifty-ninth birthday.

As painful as it all was, from the voicemail to the phone call, from the drive down to the doctor's office, there was numbness. I didn't know it then, but the coming four days were going to be the most heartbreaking yet beautiful moments of my life. World-crushing, yet somehow beautiful.

DAI DICTIONARY

Mam – like a mother, but more Welsher.

The Matrix – if I need to explain this one, what simulated reality have you been living in?

Chuck Bartowski – geeky laptop fixer by day, smooth spy guy by night.

Chuck Norris – ginger guy with a beard, knows his way round a roundhouse kick and watch out for those nunchucks.

PRAYER

Hydrate me Lord, living well.
Boost me up with every vitamin in the alphabet and
then get the same round in again.
'Cos I need it and right now – I don't understand it.

Let's face it – those nutrients were never going to cut it.
Like treating an organ rupture with a plaster
Or taking a couple Nurofen® for pneumonia

If it's "express" or not
    If it's fast-acting or not
        It's going to fall short.

The situation that's around me
    This pain, it astounds me.
        The numbness, it surrounds me

Father, please remember Dad –
            I love him and he's family.

RE: PRAYER

(what I think God was saying back)

As tough and as rough as right now feels
    You need to know I'm right there, with you in it.
        The pain you feel, I feel too.
            The news that knocked you for six
That's taken its toll on you
    Has taken its toll on Me too.

I'm here,
    I'm near
        I'm online
            Close by.

And when grappling with the news seems too large
    Remember I'm here for you and I'm still in charge.

You love your dad, but so do I.
    And when you cry
        Know that so do I.

"Jesus wept."

John 11:35

"... when we weep, he weeps with us."

(http://spoken-truth.com/john1135/)

I REMEMBER

STEALTHILY SHUFFLING NURSES
BULKY LAZYBOY ARMCHAIR
ICE LOLLIES THE SNEAKY
SHOWER THE FALSE ALARMS
THE FRIEND OF A FRIEND
EXCEEDED EXPECTATIONS
12th ROUND FIGHTING
CALON LÂN SONGS
FINAL WORDS
FINAL MOMENTS

Chapter
2

I REMEMBER

4 days.
96 hours.
5,760 minutes.
345,600 seconds.

To say that those four days were tough is an understatement. Like saying Wales has a couple of hills or that Usain Bolt has running potential.

To see your father rapidly deteriorate in front of you is like knowing the final score before the ref's blown the whistle. I saw it all unfold before my very eyes and knew the throbbing truth: there was nothing I could do to change what was going to happen. That was hard to stomach.

Pretty swiftly after being given the news, we were allocated our own room on the ward. Six of us, a couple of chairs, and Dad propped up with an array of pillows. At first small talk seemed the easiest solution, a joke shared, a story told. I don't know if you've ever had to have a difficult conversation with someone, but starting it is the hardest part, isn't it? You start by dancing your way around the edges, talking about the weather or local traffic [insert hotbed area for congestion near you; for me it's the Newport tunnel]. You're not actually paying that much attention to what the other person's saying, like a bidder at the final stages on eBay, it's just about figuring out when to make your move. Then you arrive at that moment. When small talk has finished, and both parties have contributed to the conversation. Then arrives... a comfortable silence, the perfect opportunity to change gear. But you bottle it and, instead, really hammer home about that hotbed area for congestion [remember? Newport tunnel for me].

But you do eventually get round to it, don't you? That potentially #awkward bit. In this particular instance, having only days left with my father, there was no manual for how to make that smooth transition from one depth of conversation to another. It was more like a fumbled cannonball off a diving board: not pretty, but with everything on the line "bottling it" was never a likely outcome, only diving into the deep end.

We didn't know how long we had with Dad, so threw our inhibitions out of the window, put our cards on the table, and any other metaphor you want to use. We shared. I'm so thankful I had the chance to tell Dad I loved him. I had told him a few times before but now, to hold his hand, eyeball him with tears rolling down my face, and show him how much I meant it... that was massive.

I must confess, these four days sort of merge together into one memory for me with key moments sticking out.

I REMEMBER

I remember the nurses stealthily shuffling into our room what I can only describe as bulky lazyboy armchairs (hospital-style), so we'd be that bit more comfy as I refused to leave Dad in the night and Cath refused to leave my side.

I remember the sneaky shower I had in Dad's en suite bathroom after the nurses witnessed my near breakdown from emotional exhaustion and sleep deprivation, having been by Dad's side for three days straight.

I remember Auntie Marian and Uncle Chris taking the evening shift of supporting Dad so that we could go anywhere where there wasn't a ward, hospital bed, or hand sanitizer dispenser.

I remember Mam, Cath, and I discussing the impending reality of a funeral as I jotted down notes on my iPhone over a bar meal.

I remember a friend of a friend offering us a place to stay around the corner from the hospital, just so Cath and I could get some shut-eye. I remember the clichéd Welsh weather beating down on the windscreen, us driving in the wrong direction because we'd entered the wrong postcode into the satnav. We were so far gone, not just in distance but in emotional and physical exhaustion, that it's a wonder we even got there (though I now know that God was keeping us safe, despite my idiotic driving).

I remember us all being together in the room. Dad was quiet, conserving his energy just to take a beating from this horrific disease, every so often asking for water to hydrate his drying mouth. Then there was that moment I drove to Tesco's in Carmarthen in the early hours of the morning to buy Dad iced lollies to soothe said drying mouth. Walking around that vast and empty 24-hour supermarket was certainly an out-of-body experience. Going down aisle after aisle searching for rocket lollipops, the very same you had as a kid in the summer holidays when summer was actually "summer" and not just an ironic statement. I still haven't been able to enter that supermarket since Dad died – I've waited in the car as Cath has done a shop. I've been to the petrol station a couple of times, but never the shop. It's left me with a scar I still carry today. More on that later.

I remember Dad exceeding even the doctors' expectations of how long he would stay with us. How he nodded when I said he was fighting to show us how much he loved us. All of his life Dad was a fighter, and though he lost this fight, he certainly took the cancer around the ring to the twelfth round.

I remember the false alarms. The several times when the nurses and doctors thought this was it… and Dad pulled through.

I remember Dad faintly telling me he was scared. Such a beautiful moment of vulnerability from a man who had been trained to see vulnerability as a weakness.

I remember Cath singing over him his favourite song, "Calon Lân"*.

I remember a good friend and church Elder praying over Dad and anointing him with oil, and another having *sgrws gyda Tad yn Cymraeg*.*

I remember the prayers and the Bible verses. The promises spoken of a better life on the other side. Then there were the promises I made to Dad when it was just us in the room, me saying I wanted to step up and be a fighter just as he was.

I remember that Dad in his dying moments still had better hearing than my amazing mother.

I remember that some of Dad's final words were that he wanted to find a good home for his adjustable electric bed. We laughed and cried in the same breath as we told him that this wasn't something for him to be concerned about in these moments! (FYI Dad, the bed's safe and sound in my bedroom and Cath and I love it!)

I remember the final moments. Where Jess, Dylan, Cath, Mam, and I knew "this" was it. That moment when all life seemed to have gone, and all that was left were breaths with longer gaps in between. I remember Mam suggesting that maybe we leave him; perhaps he didn't want us to see him pass. At that moment I remember so vividly life re-entering his whole being and a clenched grip as if to say, "Don't you dare, I need you with me." So we stayed and I thanked God that I knew I was exactly where I was supposed to be.

I'm sure there were many other things worthy of being remembered, but as I search my mind these are the moments that I recall. Sometimes I find it frustrating that I don't remember everything with crystal-clear precision. In a "convenient" world maybe I would have "journaled" them all down so I had archives of memories to look back on, instead of a haze of pictures, feelings, and conversations which seem so muddled. But that would never have been possible – before my grief I loved to write, but in the thick of it I couldn't think of anything worse, especially if the chapter heading was the man himself. But that's OK. ☺

DAI DICTIONARY

"Calon Lân" – Welsh hymn asking God to give us a "Pure Heart".

"*Sgrws gyda Tad yn Cymraeg*" – this is Elvish, from *Lord of the Rings*. Roughly translates to "having a conversation with Dad in Welsh".

PRAYER

I remember but I don't
I want to remember but need to forget
Just for a bit.
Just until I can get to grips with it.

God – I remember You watched Your Son give up His spirit.
I reach out to You because I know that You get it.

I remember but I don't
I want to remember but need to forget.
Just for a bit
Just until I get to grips with it.

RE: PRAYER

You're right. I've been there.
I'm the Father
I saw my perfect Son nailed to a cross
I was in so much pain I could barely watch.

I'm the Son
I chose to lay myself down
Humiliated with skin pierced thorns as my crown

And I'm the Spirit
I resurrected the Son
Third day
Tomb empty,
Battle for restoration won

I am the Triune God
And I truly get your pain.
I'm here for you
Hear what I'm saying

You may not remember, but I do
And I also see your future
and know you'll pull through.

*"The Lord has remembered us; he
will bless us; he will bless the house
of Israel; he will bless the house of
Aaron"*

Psalm 115:12

YOU ARE THERE WITH ME
THOUGH I'M HALF NUMB
I KNOW YOUR
CLOSENESS
SURROUNDS ME
DON'T DO IT IN YOUR
OWN STRENGTH
DO IT IN MINE
WHEN YOU CAN'T RUN
ANY FURTHER
I'LL PICK YOU UP
AND CARRY YOU OVER THE LINE

Chapter
3

NEXT OF KIN

After Dad passed, I experienced a mixture of emotions. He had literally fought until his final breath and although I was so sad to see him go, it was also a relief. A relief to think, "He's no longer in any pain."

Grief is a funny and complex emotion. Perhaps you feel slightly uncomfortable that I'm admitting that? Actually admitting that the passing of my father was a relief. But it was, because I knew that for a man who had endured so much physical pain over the course of his life, and then for that pain to be taken to another level over the course of those four days, there was to be no more suffering.

After more moments of tears and *cwtches** I entered the next phase. Next of kin. The phase of making everything official. In some moments I excelled. After having taken such an emotional battering from something out of my control, I could now take back some control.

I made lists and, with help from my amazing family, cooked up ideas to give a great man a great send-off. The funeral directors managed to get hold of the Welsh Guards' emblem to drape over Dad's coffin with Dad's beret resting on top. We played a clip from *Blackadder** (*Goes Forth*) and gave Baldrick* the floor as he conveyed the subject matter of war so poetically. Cath and two friends sang "I Am Coming, Lord", only accompanied by their harmonies, and then Cath sang "Calon Lân", the very song which Dad had asked her to sing at his funeral years before. Ali, my sister-in-law and fellow creative, read out a poem that I had written a couple of years before, which I had declared over Dad in those last days.

I remember walking into the bank to close down his accounts. Some of the kiosk girls were taken aback that a man who had brought so much joy even in his hardships, a man younger than some of them, was no longer with us.

Nothing can prepare you for that moment in life when you have to cancel your deceased father's direct debits. It's so interesting to remember the responses of the call centre workers. Some were very professional, as if they had handled other calls just like it. Some were apologetic and a little awkward; others came across cold-hearted, as if they were more fussed about clocking off at the end of the day rather than being your counsellor. I must confess, I preferred the awkward, apologetic ones.

There was also the matter of a shed which Dad had bought that sat proudly in the garden of his formerly council-owned bungalow. What do you do with an £800 shed that's no longer needed? Well you don't just leave it, that's a given! My father-in-law Gary, Emz my mate, and Dad's best friend Al sought to take it down so it could be picked up and put back up for a few hundred quid somewhere else.

Then there was signing the death certificate, which had to be copied and sent off to prove I wasn't pulling a fast one on Dad's life insurance cover. More phone calls, flower picking, flicking through the crem pamphlet for which option to choose in displaying Dad's resting place.

You know, shouldering the weight of "next of kin" caused two different responses in me. In the long term, it was like a kidney punch to a man who was struggling to stay standing. But in the short term it's what helped me to stay standing for as long as I did.

DAI DICTIONARY

Cwtches – plural of *cwtch*. A totally epic cuddle with a Welsh accent.

Blackadder – historical tributes through British witty sarcasm. Ben Elton before *Popcorn*, Rowan Atkinson before *Bean*, Hugh Laurie before *House*, Stephen Fry before *QI*.

Baldrick – in my mind one of the greatest poets of our time. Tony Robinson had a cunning plan before *Time Team*. Search on YouTube for Baldrick's poem called "The German Guns".

PRAYER

Next of kin,
　　The job title thing.

It's a big weight demand,
And it gives and takes with the very same hand.

Father, the form filling, the phone calling, the constant
driving
Is it steering me to exhaustion or keeping me going?
I'm thankful for control in the midst of chaos
　　but why can't it be simpler?
　　　　And less of a cost?

"Is this all really happening?"
　　Hear me,
　　　　I beg.
The tank's close to empty and I'm running on dregs.

God I know
　　You are there with me.
Though I'm half numb I know Your closeness surrounds
　　　　　　me

In this and every coming instance,
　　I ask of You
　　　　Stay close despite my distance.

RE: PRAYER

Keep going, you're doing great.
I know how you feel, every state.

Know you're not alone
'Cos when you call up these companies
I AM – at the other end of the phone.

You're surrounded by love,
From Me and others
Know that I'm here for you like no other.

Don't do it in your strength.
Do it in Mine.
When you can't run any further
I'll pick you up and carry you over the line.

Chapter 3

Next of kin –
You're carrying the weight meant for someone older
But yoke yourself to Me
You'll be more burden free
As I carry yours onto my shoulder

You feel the burden of choices
and far away from harmony,
But know Dad's not lost
He's adopted into My family.

You may be head of your own kingdom
But I'm head of Creation
Know you'll make it in spite of hardships
'Cos I'm in the business of restoration.

"Come near to God and he will come near to you."

James 4:8 (NIV)

"Counting Down the Hours" from *Poetry in Motion*

I'm counting down the hours 'til I'm home.
'Til the realm of sin ceases to exist, but we exist in the realm of perfection.

Brokenness gets fixed
And pain gets ripped off like a plaster that's eternally disposed of.

A place where burdens are lifted, dismantled, and returned.
A place filled to the brim with His glory, a place where eternity to praise Him won't seem like long enough.

Broken bodies get a Holy revamp
And blemishes are blotted out by the love of and for the Trinity.

I'm counting down the hours 'til I'm home dry,
Where I'm judged "righteous" 'cos Jesus took my place as accused in the court before the Father.

I'm eagerly awaiting paradise
Where tears only flow out of overwhelming awe and joy,
Where wars end
Where pain stops
Where burdens are lifted
And baggage is taken off our shoulders.

I'm counting down the hours 'til that day.
The day when I'm home,
Home dry.

But 'til that day,
I count every hour as time to give your name the praise.

Every hour, minute, and second
A time to be salt and light.

I count every hour a time to start the fixing process that
you'll ultimately finish.
'Cos until I'm home,
I set up camp,
'Cos there's work to be done
And every hour counts.

That being said, Lord – count me in.

TEXTS,
FACEBOOK MESSAGES
AND CARDS
SOME WITH KISSES,
OTHERS WITH
SCRIPTURE VERSES,
SOME WITH WISE WORDS,
OTHERS WITH
"I HAVE
NO WORDS"

Chapter
4

PRAYERS, TEXTS AND TEARS

"I lost my dad when I was young too..."

There seems to be some camaraderie between those who have lost people dear to them. An understanding, a knowledge that in the face of what you're going through, others have been through the same and come out the other side. I don't know whether it's fair or not, but your default position is to attach more weight to what these people say than those who haven't suffered loss. It's not that I didn't value thoughts, comments, or prayers from those who hadn't been through what I recently had, especially as I realize more and more that so many people have suffered in some way, often in ways I cannot relate to. But when I was in the company of someone I knew had suffered as I had – it almost didn't matter what they said or didn't say because what emerges is a shared suffering and that in itself can be a great comfort.

I remember a month or two after Dad had died, being in church. A man I knew, probably in his fifties, came up to me and said that he'd lost his father when he was young too. "If you ever want to talk, just know I'm here – any time," he said, as his eyes filled up behind their glasses. I've seen him many times since, and although I never took him up on that offer, I cannot stress enough how helpful the comment was. To know that, if I needed it, I could turn to him was in itself a little lifeline. Like an unopened basic first-aid kit, sitting in a cupboard next to the dried herbs and spices. If something does happen, if I need it – I know it's there.

Prayers, texts, and tears

Texts, Facebook messages, and cards. Some with kisses, others with Scripture verses, some with wise words, others with "I have no words".

I trained as an actor in Uni and one of the things I'm used to doing is performing on a stage. Sometimes to thousands, while other times if you included me, I'd be doubling the audience (well, not far off). No matter where I am or what I'm doing, after my stint I always get a buzz if my phone… you know… buzzes. "Maybe it's a text from ___?" "Wonder what they thought of it?"

Now, I know I don't get my worth from what people think, but sometimes as a performer, it's hard not to – it's like a fix.

When Dad died and the news found its way into people's lives, suddenly the richness of receiving those texts meant so much more. Depending on my mood I would either be thankful for them or simply discard them as "token condolences".

Even now I may text someone and see that the last text I received from them was a condolence. That's one of the funny things about grief, you don't always know when it's going to make an entrance. You have the big dates – the anniversaries and birthdays which invite themselves round and come knocking whether you want them to or not. But at least you can prepare for those days, you know when the day's coming, you can psych yourself up, be ready. Other times grief doesn't give any warning, it just shows up and catches you totally unawares.

———————————

Like a buffalo in a pair of boxers...

In the early hours of one morning a few years ago, Cath and I were woken up by some strange sounds mixed and produced by the front door. It was a wooden door in a house largely laid out with wooden floorboards and so the sound, like a twenty-something with a TripAdvisor app, travelled.

It sounded like someone was trying to break in. Cath and I shared glaring stares with lots of eyebrows. During the eyebrow exchange Cath said, "Is someone trying to break in?"

Kids, disclaimer here – don't try this at home. Without thinking I jumped out of bed and thundered down my sanded wooden stairs towards the front door with my hands clenched in fists. Whoever this burglar was, he wasn't going to catch me with my trousers down... it was impossible, I wasn't wearing any. It was pitch-black and my heart was pounding as I prepared to fight off this burglar in my boxers.

Then the sounds from the other side of the door stop.

Yeah, I'm thinking – *I've frightened him off* (or her – this is certainly no time to be prejudiced to burglars).

And then, out from the silence and from the other side of the door comes another sound. This one was of a sheepish Llanelli accent...

"Uh... Dafs? ... Everything alright mate?"

Turns out it was my best pal Ads and he was trying to encourage his wedding invite to quietly make its way through our letterbox. As it turned out, it wasn't that quiet, but then neither was the recipient, who hurtled down those steps like a buffalo hurtles through wild pastures... Only difference was I was in my boxers.

We still laugh about that moment to this day and it was funny because it was so unexpected. One thing I want to say to those who are going through grief and to those walking alongside grievers is this: expect Grief to be both an expected and unexpected visitor.

The formula for condolence

"An odd by-product of my loss is that I'm aware of being an embarrassment to everyone I meet. At work, at the club, in the street, I see people, as they approach me, trying to make up their minds whether they'll 'say something about it' or not. I hate it if they do, and if they don't."

(*A Grief Observed*, C. S. Lewis)

A Grief Observed, by the both literary and literally great C. S. Lewis, has been a book that I've found extremely helpful. In it Lewis comments on how he found people's responses to his grief. Some would apologize and others would skirt around it, and either way, C. S. Lewis' inner monologue would never deem it good enough. To paraphrase, if they said something, you'd think – "Why do I have to go through the formalities of how I'm feeling yet again?" Or if they didn't say anything – "Why didn't they bring it up? Don't they care?"

Reading this brought both relief and hope that I wasn't alone, and a much-needed smirk to my face. The reason being that no matter what people say, sometimes, when you're grieving, you'll manage to find something wrong with it!

Like a generous postman, instead of bills and "sorry we missed you" cards, people posted cards and chocolate through the door to say they were there if I needed them but understood I may need space.

With others, I'd be handing down furniture to friends, making space for what I'd inherited from Dad, and amongst the Chuckle Brother* "To me? To yous" were short words of, "Sorry mate, anything we can do, just let us know."

The after-service line-up

Then there's the moment after the funeral service. That wedding-like line-up of greetings and condolences. That moment when you see a pic 'n' mix of people you wouldn't see in the same place unless you happened to be in that Hugh Grant film* (not *Notting Hill* or *Love Actually*, the other one). Aunties, friends, cousins – yes, of course, but also those relatives you didn't realize were relatives, the ones who remember you when you were knee-high to a grasshopper but you've got no clue who they are – as far as you know they could be Spartacus* or even the Stig.* (Some people say she milks goats in the Himalayas, that she carves award-winning ice sculptures of Harry from One Direction,* and that she once got caught wearing double denim. All we know is, she's my third auntie twice removed.)

> Some people, teary-eyed, finding the whole experience too much to deal with would hug me and move on.

> Some would speak affirming words of how proud Dad would be of me and make *me* teary-eyed.

> Some would tell me how I'm a spit of my old man.

> Some would congratulate me on my eulogy and say how I'd summed up Dad to a tee.

> Some people would make a joke about the fact that they have no idea what to say and then just hug me.

With some people there would be the awkward cheek kiss or hug routine. You know the one where you lean in, sometimes misjudge it, and end up kissing their earlobe. It was even worse when my lovely late Mamgu was alive. I'd go in for the cheek but her kisses were like homing missiles locked on to the lips! Like Maverick in *Top Gun** I'd attempt basic evasion manoeuvres but to no avail. (Sorry, #randomtangentleavingstrangeimageinyourhead)

Back to the day of the funeral: however interesting the line-up may have been, in both services I can honestly say how thankful I am to those who humbly contributed, showed up, and paid tribute to an amazing man.

Praying for you

On my first day back at work I sat down at that same desk where I had had "that" conversation with the hospital on "that" Monday morning. There was a card with my name on it. I opened it up and in it was a short message saying sorry for my loss, that I was in this family's prayers, and there was also a comforting Scripture verse.

It was from someone in my church called Abby. She'd obviously been into my office after a Sunday morning service and had just discreetly popped it on my desk for my return. I didn't know Abby that well, though we'd crossed paths a few times as she provided prayer support for an Alpha course I was running, but I have to say, that simple act of kindness and condolence stuck with me. I remember feeling so moved, so touched.

I was blessed to be in many people's thoughts and prayers. People gave up of themselves to try and support me. Cath for one was a complete rock. But what I've learned from that one card is this – **simple things matter**. They make a difference. When you're grieving, you don't always show your gratitude, maybe you're all consumed with heartache, unable to express emotion, or just focusing your energy on holding it together. But it does matter.

Maybe it's a text, a hug, a pat on the back, chocolate through the post, or a card on the desk.

Maybe it's leaving space for choked-up out-loud thinking, or recognizing when you need distracting with a beer and a few racks of pool.

To those who walk alongside those who grieve – thank you for how you give of yourself in spite of yourself. It does *not* go unnoticed.

To those who walk close by to grievers – you may not be in the thick of it with us, but you see our pain too. And thank you, because like I said – those simple things matter.

DAI DICTIONARY

Chuckle Brother – slapstick, slips, and catchphrases with the inevitable bucket of water over someone's head. If you're not having a nostalgia moment – get on the YouTube!

That Hugh Grant film – surely you got this one? Four beddings and a mural (*Four Weddings and a Funeral*).

I'm Spartacus – apparently anyone can be Spartacus, you just need to stand up and say it with conviction.

The Stig – that bloke off *Top Gear* with a white helmet on. It's unfortunate he's wearing it; you can't tell what he looks like. He could be anyone.

One Direction – if you're looking for me to describe this one, you're looking in the wrong direction.

Top Gun – if Tom Cruise with aviators doesn't bring back fond memories, you've lost that loving feeling.

Comms runner – during World War II there would be comms runners (communications runners) who would pass vital information from officers to the soldiers on the front line. They weren't where the action was most intense, but were still very important soldiers. Check out *Band of Brothers*, there are some in that.

PRAYER

God,
Thank You for generous postmen
For the texts of comfort
And the cards of compassion.

Thank You for the frontline soldiers – those who are with me,
beside me and behind me.
With these comrades I make it through another day.
And thank You for the messengers
For the *"comms"* runners* who bring poignant prayers
and fresh supplies of Scripture.

RE: PRAYER

I am with you.
   Always.
I'm in your Bible
   And the other side of your prayers.
My Spirit has made His home inside you
   I'm with you.
But I'm also present in My servants
   I'm in those texts,
In their words
   or lack of words.
I'm in the Scriptures they send
   And the cards they pen.
Often they're spot on,
   Sometimes not.
But their hearts are for you
   And I'm in their hearts.
So their hearts are in the right place

Know that I am here.
   I am with you.
      And know that I'm not going anywhere.

"Blessed be the God and Father of our Lord Jesus Christ, the Father of mercies and God of all comfort, who comforts us in all our affliction, so that we may be able to comfort those who are in any affliction, with the comfort with which we ourselves are comforted by God."

2 Corinthians 1:3–4

THE WAVES OF
PRESSURE
WHICH I HAD
ONCE SURFED ON
WERE NOW
CRASHING
OVER
ME
AND
THROWING ME
UNDER

Chapter 5

EMPTY SHOPPING BAGS AND BLOSSOM TREES

From "to-do" lists to "can't-do" lists

The first few weeks of grief I was kept running by people's messages of love, Scripture, and prayer, be it in text or person. It was really helpful. With lots of stuff to organize there was plenty to be preoccupied with. Daily contact with the funeral directors, swinging by government offices to pick up birth certificates, picking themes and colours from the florist to name a few.

The funeral gave me something to focus my mind on. It became something to work to and that, matched with the initial relief that Dad was no longer suffering, helped me to find a bit of a groove. I had a couple of weeks' compassionate leave which was really helpful and it took that long to sort out the funeral. After that it was back to work with a big "to-do" list waiting for me.

When I say big, I mean caps lock BIG. I was writing an outreach show called "the coffee shop tour" to go on a tour of churches. All the venues had already been booked. I was also about to perform a C. S. Lewis adaptation with Cath to a horde of primary school kids called "The Tiger, the Snitch and the Chest of Drawers" (it was going to be a re-tour of the first play I had written. Oh and the title? Well, it's called tiger 'cos it's like a stripy lion, snitch 'cos it sounds like witch, and then get this bit, it's going to blow your mind – instead of calling the magical piece of furniture which gets you to Narnia the wardrobe, I thought I'd mix it up a bit and call it the chest of drawers. Crazy eh?). On top of all that, I was due to be performing on the main stage at Spring Harvest* both mornings and evenings, with an after-hours show to boot.

So, as I think I've just established, there was a lot going on and I was lacking in time to prep. I knew that I wasn't 100 per cent when I returned to work but I think the rhythm of giving Dad a good send-off had lulled me into a false sense of security. Just to add to the mix, everything was changing at work too – the charity I worked for was merging with another charity, and I was getting a new line manager.

I remember working on the coffee shop tour in an unfamiliar Starbucks, carving out ideas in my notebook with a heightened awareness that I was out of my depth. With the ever-increasing to-do list and an ever-decreasing time limit to meet it, I was struggling to stay buoyant, I was struggling to keep my head above water. It was all too much, too soon. **The waves of pressure which I had once surfed on were now crashing over me and throwing me under.**

I felt a face twitch appear. I felt my breathing becoming deeper and more accentuated. I felt like there was no way out. No way forward.

I spoke to Cath, who was pretty tired and stressed herself, totally understandably with all she had put out for me – it was like she put her own agenda on hold. At first she didn't realize, but then she did. She spoke to Paul

– friend, church leader, and spiritual dad - who helped me make a path through all the pressure. We cancelled the C. S. Lewis tour, and streamlined the Spring Harvest responsibilities, keeping what caused me the least anxiety. And beyond all of that, my gorgeous wife and team of epic colleagues took on my big project of the year – the coffee shop tour – sending curveballs of problems out of the park with a baseball bat of solutions. Suddenly, with fewer plates to spin everything felt that much more manageable. And breathe!

Spring had cancelled last minute

Spring Harvest came and went and went down well. People stepped in to fill in the gaps, and the stuff I performed with the comically on time Lucy Thampi was well received. The highlight was a parody of a parody originally parodied by the Two Ronnies* – the "answering the question before last" Mastermind sketch. (You can check it out here – https://www.youtube.com/watch?v=zaoGAp1TKTA)

The vast majority of people were so helpful. Sympathetic yes, but people also gave me space to feel normal and crack the occasional "funny" joke too. My storytelling friend Bob Hartman ended up taking on my after-hours show and with no pressure he invited me to be a guest artist to do some of my poetry bits. After some deliberation, I accepted. I got to the venue and there was a bit of confusion as my name was still on the programme since I had pulled out last minute. I remember one steward – nice enough, but for this story I will refer to him as "Mr Foot In-mouth".

"I don't know what's happening tonight; apparently the other guy pulled out last minute, yeah some bloke called Dai Woolridge – though I've never even heard of the guy!" he said, or words to that effect. Unbeknownst to him he was talking to said "some bloke called Dai Woolridge".

I changed the subject pretty quickly because I didn't want him to feel bad. Alright – part of me did want him to feel bad. Cards on the table, part of me wanted to say…

"The reason that guy you've never heard of pulled out of his after-hours show is because he's probably on the edge of burnout after going through the most horrendous two months of his life. But hey, sorry it's put you out."

I'm glad I didn't say anything. Why would I expect him to know the ins and outs of my personal life? (How could he? He didn't even know who I was!) ☺

After all, it's not like I've never put my foot in it, is it? Though perhaps I could've agreed with him and said, "I don't know, amateurs these days. If you ever want a true professional, get in touch", followed by a swift revealing of my business card which reads "Dai Woolridge: poet, storyteller, griever". Showed that hand again, didn't I? Oops.

Doctor, Doctor –

I feel like this is the beginning of one of those Doctor, Doctor jokes… (It's not, don't worry.)

As it turned out, Spring Harvest was manageable. Because I knew exactly what I needed to do, I had enough in the tank to do it. I rounded it all off performing a couple of poems in Cath's after-hours session and we got back in the early hours of the morning. Just a few hours later, the sun rose and I was back at work running a schools workshop on mental health. I remember another out-of-body experience, as I ran through the symptoms of anxiety and depression to a year group of fourteen-year-olds. What I was teaching felt uncomfortably familiar. Yes, I'd managed Spring Harvest, but I was still tired and hyper-aware that I just wasn't right.

I got back to the office to a meeting with my new line manager. There was a flip chart, targets, numbers, and even talk of a new office. After two minutes, I'd stopped listening.

It took everything in me to hold it together. He encouraged me to take my time but at that point, on the brink of breaking, to me, they were words with good intentions but they offered little comfort. At the close of the meeting I found a free room, closed the door, and broke down. Like a heart-breaking game of hide and seek Cath found me and held me amongst the streaming tears. That was the moment I really knew three certain words…

I managed to book in to see the doctor, was it that day? The day after? I can't remember, but I close another door behind me.

"What can we do for you today?" said the doctor, or words to that effect.

I gave the headline news of losing my dad, that I'd gone back to work but that perhaps it was too soon and I needed more time. I may have even talked tablets.

As soon as I mentioned my loss his demeanour shifted, but he kept on asking questions. How was I doing? Why did I think I needed more time? I started to get more choked up as I fumbled my way through the answers. He pressed a little more, as if I wasn't getting to the crux of the matter. Why? But why?

Because… because three words.

"I'm. Not. Well."

It might have felt like an unfair interrogation at the time but as soon as I said those three words I understood *why*. It wasn't for him to tell me what I was or wasn't feeling at that time – he could have said something but it would have had less of an impact. Before that moment, I'd been trying to ignore it. The doctor saw it, but I had failed to fully accept it myself. The self-realization that I could no longer keep on keeping on, that the tank was officially empty – that I was not well. I felt a big burden lift off my shoulders and a lightness around my chest for the first time in I didn't know how long.

Empty shopping bags and blossom trees

With time off work, I could operate at a different pace – whatever pace I wanted. I put together a gallery of photos, medals, and memorabilia to remember Dad by. I had lie-ins, escaped into box sets, and attacked chocolate like a predator on an Attenborough programme.* And although I had 'fessed up to those three words, this was still scratching the surface into my grief journey. There were ongoing next of kin "to-do" lists.

By themselves, they might not have been big things, but they built up, and like adding to a Jenga* tower, the more they built, the more unstable they got. I still had a plethora of "Dad stuff" that didn't fall into the categories of "chuck" or "charity shop".

Clothes that still smelled of Dad. Dad's phone and wallet. Clothes that I could wear which I later found out were too hard to wear. I even had a special section of eBay items, pricey designer brands Dad had bought which hadn't long left their sealed packaging.

There was also a drawer in the utility room with all of Dad's correspondence. Lots of letters addressed to Dad – important stuff that kept adding to the Jenga pile, as his mail was redirected to our place.

The crem bit...

Then, [insert sarcasm] my most favourite experience of all – with the crematorium. Let's back up a bit first. Dad didn't mind talking about his preferred eventualities after his death and to be fair it made our job a little easier.

"I don't want to be worm food," he used to say. And as his Mam, Dad, and long-term girlfriend Tracey had found rest in a local crem, he was pretty happy with that as his resting place too.

I made the phone call...

"Hi, I recently had a service for my dad with you – the funeral directors said I could contact you about getting a memorial."

She's nice enough. She tells me there's some catalogue where I can choose the tree I want. Right enough, a couple of days later I'm looking through the catalogue and I call back.

This time it's a guy.

"Hi, I spoke with [insert name], is she there?"

"No. She's broken her arm." (Or maybe her leg... There was a cast involved, I remember that much.)

"Of course she has," I think to myself.

(I end up going through the same spiel as last time.)

"Oh. You want a tree?" he says.

"Yes, please," I say.

And then comes the fun list of options.

What type of tree? How long do you want the tree? (In time, not inches.) Where would you like the tree situated?

Now. At this point I had had enough of making decisions, especially decisions relating to Dad. I wanted a tree to remember him by, simple, isn't it? I didn't want to get stuck in the detail or bat answers back from questions – just give me a tree!

I end up visiting the place (the woman's still off with a broken limb). I pick a place and a tree, it was a blossom tree – what Dad would have wanted. Then there's a plaque to inscribe – more decisions and more words to write. I'm running on empty but I come up with this and everyone seems happy...

"Dad you are so loved and you will be so missed."

Right, job done you're thinking? No. How could I be so careless? Of course, I have to think about chippings... size of chippings, colour of chippings, the lack of chippings? I go for cream, small-to-medium chippings. He then tells me the day to visit when it's all done.

I do. I travel an hour, my first time back to the place where I had finally said goodbye to Dad's earthly body, but the tree's not ready – there aren't even any chippings! I try and dispute this fact but by now I'm on the brink of burnout. The guy gets defensive and a little shirty – no apology, it gets awkward. Cath defuses the situation.

And as he takes us to the tree, he starts offloading on us about how he's going on holiday because if you're stuck in "this" place too long, you'll go mad. As I'm sure you can imagine [insert sarcastic reading tone], my heart "went out" to him.

Maybe it doesn't seem like much to you but at that

time, in my state – it was.

I had been through the most difficult ordeal of my life and to top it off I was dealing with a guy who wasn't overly fussed on being helpful. I'm sure he's had better days at the office but this wasn't one of them.

Shopping in spacesuits

The load kept building. I remember it all getting too much for me.

It got to the point where I could no longer open letters, as if my subconscious had gone on strike and shut off my letter-opening skills before it joined the picket line.

The simple task of picking a tree for Dad became to me more difficult than bringing Apollo 13* home was to NASA. It may have burned up in re-entry but I was burning out and shutting down.

I'd visit supermarkets and have semi-panic attacks thinking of making yet another list, having yet another responsibility to shoulder. For crying out loud – a simple food shop! Imagine that? Sounds ridiculous doesn't it? To think that buying an iceberg lettuce, a couple of tomatoes, and one of those posh ready meals would cause me to leave the supermarket, and the basket's contents, halfway through a shop and just sit in the car. But for me those supermarkets were a double-edged sword – they'd confront me with the fact that after the decision making of being next of kin, I could no longer make decisions – no matter if those decisions had barcodes. Couple that with the vivid picture of "that" time, searching Tesco's supermarket for rocket lollipops to grant a man you love his dying wish, and it doesn't matter how many Clubcard points you get for it – in this instance, every little doesn't help.

As I conclude this chapter, I want to address a few things. To those who are grieving, know that it's OK. Maybe you've picked up a twitch or a stammer. Maybe you're more OCD than you ever were, maybe the most normal activity triggers for you the biggest Everest that you feel you can't climb. Maybe it's all of the above or a completely different list altogether. In whatever case, know that what you're going through is normal and know that someone else has probably gone through it too. But perhaps, just as I have shared, maybe you need to consider help. To quote my doctor, "It's OK – you're not Superman." (Or to paraphrase the doc – "It's OK – you're not Jesus!")

To those who walk alongside those who grieve, know that your decision to be understanding even when you don't understand is massive. When things don't go to plan, know that your flexibility to adapt to the situation is a lifeline. Cath was a flexible, problem-solving fire putter-outer, and I'm so thankful for her.

To those involved in providing services to those in grieving: we appreciate all you do to make things that little bit easier. But please, have patience with us. It may be a job for you, but for us it's a role that nothing in life can really prepare you for.

And as I look back to those moments with the crem, the guy I referred to didn't do anything horrendous, and I also recognize that he wasn't the reason for me being unwell, he was just one of the straws that broke the camel's back. And that's one of the reasons I still find it hard going to that crematorium, because I seem to remember the wrong memories. Maybe crematorium staff don't need to be leading experts in human behaviour to figure out that people who use their services might be going through a rough time. Surely a bit of empathy and leeway would help? You'd hope it came with the job description. But then I probably just caught this guy on an off day. And where some are unhelpful, I'm sure many more far exceed the roles on their contract and end up being a major blessing to those in need.

Largely, I was so blessed by those I came into contact with and am thankful for them (two nurses, one doctor, and the funeral directors in particular). Thank you to those who go out of their way to help people in grief, even if for you it's just a job. But a gentle reminder if you're reading – what you do and how you do it can play a big part in someone's grieving process, so please – listen carefully, show grace, and go easy.

DAI DICTIONARY

Spring Harvest – a Christian conference at Butlins... fewer hen parties, more praise parties.

Two Ronnies sketch – one of the classic comedy sketches by the infamous Ronnie Barker and Ronnie Corbett.

Jenga – think Leaning Tower of Pisa with little wooden blocks.

Attenborough programme – and here we see a spritely mammal of the poet species. Watch as he attempts "wit" to define a world-renowned broadcaster whom you will know anyway.

Apollo 13 – remember Kevin Bacon and Tom Hanks in space and they couldn't get back? ("Houston, we have a film reference.")

PRAYER

Father,
No more.
No more letters
No more phone calls
No more food lists and shopping baskets.
No more picking which spot or tree.
No more workload
'Cos I'm on my knees.

Can't keep running on empty
Can't keep, keep on keeping on.
I'm stopping.
My hazards are on
And I'm pulling onto the hard shoulder

Thank You for medical mechanics
Who assured me that coming to a stop is natural when
you're out of fuel.
Hand over the keys
And...... breathe!

RE: PRAYER

Pull over.
Know that recovery is on its way.
You were not made to run on an empty tank.
I'm God – and even I rested.

The "Chin up"
    "Stiff upper lip"
        And "Get on with it"
You've got to know doesn't always hack it.
Sometimes it misses what's going on under the surface.
I'm proud of you for coming to terms with it.

Now,
    Stop doing and start being.
        Know –
I'm not a list or a shopping bag
    I'm the Sustainer
        So, come to Me
            Give Me what you can.
In exchange, I'll give you something,

                    Peace which passes understanding.

"Do not be anxious about anything, but in every situation, by prayer and petition, with thanksgiving, present your requests to God. And the peace of God, which transcends all understanding, will guard your hearts and your minds in Christ Jesus."

Philippians 4:6–7 (NIV)

I'm Flat
A poem

"My hazards are on
I've worn through the rubber
And now my timing belt has buckled
under the pressure."

https://youtu.be/v6fV9hhuZCw

GOD WAS IN THE CRYING SPACES THE SILENT SPACES AND THE "I DON'T WANT TO ACKNOWLEDGE GOD" SPACES

Chapter
6

MEDS VS MEDITATION

Do you need a faith check-up if you're relying on anti-depressants to get you through the day?

Now, if ever there's a chapter that could be divisive, or create a need to get out your tightrope pumps,* it would be this one!

I mean, I'm addressing the age-old topic of reliance on God vs reliance on something or someone else. Do we seek self-sustenance or God-sustenance? I think we can safely accept that we need to lean on God in the midst of difficult times. But what does said "God leaning" look like and, for that matter, what does it **not** look like?

Over the years I've heard points made from different sides of the spectrum when it comes to the issue of faith and anti-depressants.

I've heard no-punch-pulling-preachers argue that a reliance on anything that's not God is not that godly.

And I've heard the other side of the coin too – God made it available, so if it helps, use it. If you broke your leg outside A&E, but refused to go in because you were asking God for help, wouldn't you be missing the obvious? But then what if the outworking of your faith no longer finds itself in your maker, just in your medication?

Now, maybe you can see where I'm going with this, that I'm arguing the need for balance. I'm not going to tell you otherwise, but what I do want to tell you is a bit of my personal experience on this. So much of the time we find it easy to "do faith" in principle; we have a hypothetical answer to a hypothetical question. But when the proverbial noun hits the fan it can be less easy to find that polished answer and I think that real faith requires us to be exactly that – real.

In fact my dad had been on medication for depression and Post-Traumatic Stress Disorder (PTSD). He had seen and experienced so much on the front line, patrolling the streets of Northern Ireland, facing an enemy in plain clothing, that he needed them. They helped him to control his paranoia and take the edge off, but I never thought, "Dad – are you sure you need meds?" After all that he'd been through that dilemma had never even entered my mind.

I remember being given a book on depression by a girlfriend some years ago. She had been suffering with depression and some days would be more difficult for her than others. The book argued the case that depression was a physical illness, and that statement really struck me. Hey, this is not just something we cook up in our heads through a time of self-pity. Just because it's not as visible as a broken leg doesn't mean it's any less real.

Over the years, my wife Cath has battled with her self-image, how she sees herself, and has taken medication too. For her it was anti-anxiety tablets. Even though we journeyed through her anxiety together and prayed about it, our experience has been that meds have helped, not hindered. In principle, I had seen the use of medication as something that could help people who needed that extra support, even if they did follow Jesus. That being said, I must confess I've been a bit of a hypocrite on this issue and I'll bet there are others out there, Christian or not, who'd be the same. When others have decided to take medication, I haven't viewed it as a weakness on their part, or as a lack of commitment to God. However, when it came to the decision of possibly taking them myself, I ended up in an inner battle over that same stigma – "If I take these, I've failed. I'm a Christian; I shouldn't need anything but God to sustain me, right?"

Wait a minute – it's OK for others who need it and it doesn't make them weak, but if I take them – it does? It may have been an inward dialogue, but I'm self-aware enough to know that the double standard was there.

It's not as if I wrestled with this like two bargain hunters wrestling for designer jeans in the TK Maxx modbox*, I came to my conclusion fairly sharpish. At this point in my grief – no longer riding the initial waves of "doing" – the reality of Dad's passing was really beginning to hit home in a new way altogether; I knew I needed them.

I was getting more OCD; the obsolete space between our kitchen and bathroom had become a place where stuff gathered and I could not handle it. Not in a "well, that's annoying" kind of way, but in a "if we don't tidy and organize that, it's going to break me" kind of way.

The feeling of stage fright at the thought of going into work, the inability to do a food shop or to cook, the long deep breaths in and out as if I'd just spent the last hour shredding calories in the gym. In the end, for me choosing meds wasn't a big decision – it was a thought-through, measured decision, but for me it was right. Taking them wasn't a "get-me-fixed-up-so-I-can-get-on-with-it" choice – it was a "to-get-me-through-this, I'll-take-all-the-help-I-can-get" choice.

So where does God fit into all of this? Well, He fits right in the centre, where He should. I know that it wasn't the meds that got me through, it was God. It was just that the meds were one of the ways that God provided for me practically, like He did so in other ways too – through my doctor, my grief counsellor, Cath, my mam, Auntie Marian, my church leaders, close friends, family, and missional community to name a few.

God was in the crying spaces, the silent spaces, and the "I don't want to acknowledge God" spaces. He was there through it all and although I look back and know I could have leaned on Him more, I know that every time I leaned back and lost my balance, He was there to catch me. In every silence – He was talking. In every moment – He was present, even if sometimes I felt like He wasn't, even if sometimes, I chose to ignore Him.

You see, for me I worked out that there's no issue with medication. It was for a period of time during a season of hardship. For other people, it aids an ongoing emotional/mental/physical illness like anxiety, depression, or PTSD. I have no problem with saying that during that time I was "depressed" and that I suffered with "anxiety". Neither do I have a problem admitting that since my walk through grief, I've emerged different – in many ways stronger, but I wouldn't be kidding anyone if I said **I didn't** walk with a limp. (More on this anon.)

In Christian contexts it can be difficult when we feel labelled. We have everything we could possibly want and need in God, so why should we be depressed? This is true, and as believers who have been adopted into God's family to become co-heirs with Christ, I really believe we should strive to live out this "good news" with joy-filled lives and even tell that to our faces once in a while. But joy's more than an emotional response, isn't it? It's a choice. And sometimes making that choice is really tough.

At the climax of Jesus' arrest, He went to the garden of Gethsemane. He spiritually carried the weight of the world on His shoulders and though we could never begin to understand what that would feel like, He was so anxious that understandably He sweated blood. Even still He said to the Father, "Not my will, but yours, be done" (Luke 22:42).

I don't think in that moment He was doing God a disservice by not doing Gene Kelly kick flicks off of lampposts whilst singing in the rain. Yet in the midst of His pain, He trusted the Father, He chose joy.

I think the challenge for us is to go do the same. For me, medication or meditation, pills or prayers – it doesn't have to be either/or, it can be both. Meds aren't the answer, God is, but I don't think that makes them void. Neither is it idolatry if you wear the name badge "Christian" but still take 20 mg of citalopram after your quiet time. I don't think taking meds means that they automatically take the place of God in our lives.

We're called to be obedient. To trust God even when we don't know what's happening or why it's happening. The question isn't meds or no meds, whether we take them or not, the question is: "Are we turning to God?"

After all, He is the one who will get us through.

Picture grief as a ten-foot wall in front of you.

Meds don't get you over the wall, they just stop you slipping.

God gets you over the wall – He's at the top of it because He's climbed it Himself – His arm's stretching down and He's there to pull you up.

DAI DICTIONARY

Tightrope pumps – needed by trapeze artists and those of us who embrace difficult conversations.

TK Maxx modbox – I don't really understand what this is, but Cath tells me it's full of designer clothes at bargain prices… I think she's working on commission.

Wrecking-balled – just a cheeky bit of wordplay here, with those big swinging balls that smash buildings. Thought I'd mix things up a bit and make the noun a verb. I know – nuts innit?!

PRAYER

God.
As I cling towards the wall
The meds make foot holes so I get that breather

It doesn't transform my cause
or lift me over with acrobatic parkour
But it does make it easier.

To give me time to look up and see that You're here too.
Not as a bystander
More than a supporter
But as a muddy T-shirt participator

Someone who's already climbed the wall
And someone who comes back for those who call to
You.

You are the best meds in my medicine cabinet
You're my mediator
And I do best when I meditate on You.

RE: PRAYER

If your knees are weak
And you're covered in blisters
Know I'm kitted out with a medical kit

I can't always get you from A to B with no obstacles
Not because I'm not God and Sovereign of all
It's because in this life there'll be obstacles because of
the fall

But I can promise you this...
Next time round,
On the other side
I'm preparing a place where
walls are wrecking-balled*
and obstacles obliterated

Not just that.
Know also,
As messy as this life gets
You won't walk it alone
'Cos My Son has already walked it
Not just that – but if you want it
He comes back for you –
Your arm over Him
And His over you
He'll help you cross the line.

The Lord is my shepherd; I shall not want.
    He makes me lie down in green pastures.

He leads me beside still waters.
    He restores my soul.

He leads me in paths of righteousness
    for his name's sake.

Even though I walk through the valley of
    the shadow of death,
    I will fear no evil,
for you are with me;
    your rod and your staff,
    they comfort me.

You prepare a table before me
    in the presence of my enemies;
you anoint my head with oil;
    my cup overflows.

Surely goodness and mercy shall follow me
    all the days of my life,
and I shall dwell in the house of the Lord
    for ever.

Psalm 23

I HEAR YOU
EVERY
SILENCE
EVERY PAUSE
EVERY INTAKE OF
BREATH FOLLOWED
WITH NO
WORDS

Chapter

7

SILENT PRAYERS

What to pray when nothing comes out.

Prayer words and God's word

When I think about my faith journey and the disciplines which need to be my bedrock, prayer would get my top spot. Well, joint top spot – if I suggested that God's word is paramount and of utmost importance in living out the Christian faith, I don't think I'd be called out as a heretic.

With the Bible in one hand and prayer in the other (or a Bible/prayer sandwich if you pray with your hands closed), you can form a complete dialogue with the Deity. "The Word" gives us space to hear from God, to let Him speak to us, change us, equip us, and transform us. Through these breathed-out words we learn more about God because they're HIS breathed-out words, HIS living words made alive by HIS Spirit, THE Spirit – the Holy Spirit. His words which speak of the Word who became flesh – Jesus, the hero of the story. And as we read this story, we come to find that it's a love story from the Trinity and that it was written for you and me.

As for prayer – well, that's the other side to the conversation coin, isn't it? That's talking back – sharing your deepest and surface needs, your thoughts, your questions, and your random tangents, all of it. God's up for relationship and He's not in it just to talk our ears off – He's up for us talking back and He loves it.

Learning the prayer styles

You get different styles of prayer, don't you?

1. You've got the prayer where you slip into your posh phone voice (come on, we've all done it, haven't we? Maybe it makes us that extra bit holy, who knows!).
2. There's the whispering under your breath prayers, where you're talking to God in a public place but it might not be appropriate to go all guns blazing on the normal voice. I like these prayers, though to passers-by we probably look like we're a couple of Scripture verses short of a quiet time, if you catch my drift.
3. Then there are the pause... prayers with... pauses disguised as endings. You know the ones where the prayer comes to a nice close, a silence arrives to establish the ending, but then the prayer's back in with more... pauses disguised as endings (this is an optional... pause before going to number 4).
4. You've got the watery prayers with holy filled tear ducts.
5. There's the really peaceful prayers which you can't remember because you were unconscious at the time.
6. Then there's the pack a punch with every syllable prayers. You know the ones where you're giving EVERY, WORD, a WORKOUT! I've no doubt God loves these prayers but be warned... possible side effects include whiplash.

Usually, I'll fall into the number 3 prayer camp (not literally a camp obviously. Imagine a prayer camp with a bunch of number 3s – if you prayed before supper you'd end up fasting because you wouldn't eat 'til breakfast the next morning). That being said, in my grief I picked up another prayer style – the silent prayer.

For the first two or three months after the funeral I don't know if I actually prayed... out loud I mean. There were times when I wanted to, but it almost felt physically impossible... like I didn't have it in me to pray. Was I angry with God? No, not really. Had I stopped believing in prayer? No, I continued to believe in it. It's not that I felt God had left me or stopped listening – none of the above, it was just too tough to talk.

As I think back to that time, I think the reason for my prayer struggle was due to whom I associated prayer with: Dad.

I had often prayed with Dad in those final days; I prayed for peace, I prayed for comfort, and that Dad would know God as his personal Immanuel – "God with him". I prayed silent prayers along with hand held prayers. I wasn't the only one who prayed, and neither was I some saint worthy of a stained-glass selfie to take pride of place on a church building window, but I did... pray.

And so when the moment came when Dad gave up the fight, my prayer lips got less of a workout. You see, prayer felt like an open wound and vocalizing my thoughts to God felt too sore.

As I reflect on my relationship with God during that time, I find a few small spiritual breadcrumbs left over after I opened the dialogue with the Father. I mean small, croutons at best, but they were there.

I remember some barely conscious internal dialogues with God along the lines of "Well, this sucks, doesn't it?" or "Look after him for me, will You?"

Thankfully for me, though I may not have gotten on my knees and clasped my hands on a regular basis, I knew that He knew exactly how I felt in any given moment. Not just that, but He got it – He got me and I think I subconsciously rested in that fact even through the fogginess of my grief.

The funeral prayer...

Possibly one of the hardest prayers I prayed was a written prayer two weeks to the day after Dad's passing. We had a florist who lived pretty close to Dad make up the floral tribute to rest on top of the coffin. The flowers were daffodils – some of Dad's favourite flowers and ones which reflected the man himself – born in spring and as Welsh as they come, mun!*

I remember sitting at my mam's dining table with pen in hand, hovering over the card, searching for what words to put in what order. Words are important to me and so was Dad (#obvs) – these two factors combined meant I wasn't rushing into a message reminiscent of a belated birthday card scribble as you're pulling up to the party.

Thinking back to what I wrote now, it wasn't a direct prayer because I actually wrote it to my earthly father. But that said, with each ink-placed letter I prayed the message to be true before my heavenly Father.

Earlier in this chapter I talked about the importance of prayer and reading God's word. Both are vital in our walk with God. I've taken some time to unpack the valleys of my prayer life but it was who I knew God to be through His word that gave me the courage to write this particular prayer. James 4:8 says, "Draw near to God, and he will draw near to you."

Dad had a bit of a complicated relationship with God, which I'll talk about later in this book, but I believe that whatever had happened before his last days, Dad drew near to God. And so the message tied to the daffs* resting on top of the coffin was a response to what I believed happened next – can you guess what it is yet? God drew near to Dad. It was not just wishful thinking but it was a penned prayer written with a morsel of faith in the Father that what I'd written was true. How could I know? I rest on the promise found in His word, in James 4:8.

Here's my prayer penned message, written to my earthly father because of the hope I have in my heavenly Father.

Dad, You are so loved.
    You will be so missed.
We are so glad to know that
        where you are,
Pain will be just a distant memory,
And joy will be the adjective
        for all eternity.
    Dave + Cath
        x

And with haziness I remember re-praying this truth through number 4 watery prayers – breaking-down-with-tears prayers, praying that Dad was safe and no longer in pain. Every so often, I continue to pray it.

DAI DICTIONARY

Mun – the Welsh way of ending a sentence. (Oh hang on, I didn't finish that properly.)

Mun (take 2) – the Welsh way of ending a sentence, mun. (Nailed it that time.)

Daffs – an abbrev. of daffodils.

PRAYER

RE: PRAYER

I hear you.
    Every silence.
        Every pause
Every intake of breath followed with no words.
    Know I hear them all.
        I know.
            I hear.
                So know that I AM here.

"For God alone, O my soul,
  wait in silence,
for my hope is from him."

Psalm 62:5

IN THE
THICKNESS
OF MY
SICKNESS
YOU CARRY
AND SUSTAIN
ME

Chapter 8

SICK NOTE

Burnout. It's a bit of a funny word really, isn't it? By "funny" I don't mean "haha funny", like when someone trips over a sandwich board outside a noodle bar or falls off a treadmill in a fancy fitness room (yeah, both me).

But "the B word" is an odd word. It's one of those words that the vast majority of people have an opinion on, or a definition for, but it can be tricky to share it.

It's one of those words that either is used so excessively that it loses its gravitas and ends up becoming an unintended hyperbole, or is totally unaccepted in the Christian vocabulary.

Now I don't confess to be some expert on burnout.

I don't have fancy letters before or after my name (well, apart from a BA for three years of playing drama games like "Zip, Zap, Boing"*). I didn't graduate with a first at "Burnout University".

I'm not a scholar in stress, nor a professor in post-trauma, and before you ask, no I don't have a PhD in that well-known science "burnoutology". (I always get asked that question.)

Now that I've shown my hand, I will say this – I've been

through it. As I've journeyed through grief "the B word" has been one of the stops along the way. So I think that gives me a seat at the table, even if it is one of those miniature seats which you only find in a nursery class.

I'm sure burnout is different for different people. One person could be affected in a totally different way from another. There's also a burnout spectrum, with people at varying points on the scale. However, I want to say that I think it is different from "stress".

I don't have to tell you that the vast majority of us deal with stress to some degree or other on a regular basis. You can even see it in the rhythms of everyday life, can't you? You can be stressed if you miss a deadline, if you forget to take the bins out, or if you're late for an important meeting. And it's not that stress isn't, you know, "stressful" – it's just that usually we find a way to cope.

In my little seat, with my less than fancy credentials, here's my contribution to the "burnout" conversation. Burnout happens when the stress- or anxiety-o-meter exceeds your own coping threshold. It's when something snaps – or where a temperature is so high it causes the thermometer to explode (even if you only see that happen in cartoons).

Grief was my exploding thermometer.

During the months after Dad had passed there were signals that pointed to burnout. These are some of them...

I breathed deeply when I felt uncomfortable.
The simplest task became impossible.

I couldn't handle disorder; even if it was a cubbyhole of a couple of coats and shoes that needed sorting, it would debilitate me.

I panicked when I didn't feel in control,
whereas before I had been pretty laid-back.

I couldn't deal with seeing food that was a day
past its sell-by date and the thought of cooking
food would send me into despair.

Back in those last days in the hospital, the stress and anxiety of the situation had caused me to lose about a stone in weight. Shortly after, the tide turned as I turned to comfort food – I'd munch on a bar of chocolate every evening and then also another bar in the day (and I don't mean fun-size but those big bars which are meant for sharing). My time off work also coincided with the Easter build-up and I'd often come back from Tesco's with a buy one get one free deal on Easter eggs and end up eating both... The only way I'd willingly go to a supermarket was so that I could make a beeline for the seasonal aisle. And so I found that stone that I'd previously lost, and with it, I found another one (that was a special deal put on by my own coping mechanism, "find one stone, get the other one free").

Admittedly, as habits go, stuffing your face with chocolate every day is not exactly considered hardcore, is it?

It's not like I was painting the town red, sleeping around, or taking coke (not the cola kind), but it still wasn't healthy. I didn't care about what I was eating or how much, the point was it was something I could control. Chocolate tasted good, with all the mess I'd been through and continued to feel; surely I owed myself something good? A little sugar hit, just for a bit?

The ugly head-rearers...

As I alluded to in one of my previous chapters (Empty Shopping Bags...), some of these actions and reactions are still ongoing. Only fairly recently have I got back into cooking properly, probably because cooking was something I was getting into when you know what hit the fan and my brain just made the connection. Shopping trips have been a major cause of stress for me, and in turn Cath too, probably for a course of two years after Dad passed, if not more. At the time of writing this chapter, only in the last six weeks have I actually been able to comfortably do a "weekly shop". And sometimes if I start feeling stressed or anxious, even if it's in proportion to the situation, some of these rhythms rear their ugly heads.

Why's it awkward to talk about burnout in the church?

I think this issue is addressed a lot more than it used to be, but that said there's still further progress to make.

The reality is, some people don't get what "burnout" is because they've never gone so far down a path of pressure or anxiety as to experience a "breakpoint". There's nothing wrong with this, but it can narrow people's understanding, especially if they can only relate to the issue through the lenses of their own experiences.

Sometimes unhelpful theology can hinder our understanding of burnout. Although I believe it is biblical to rejoice in our sufferings, sometimes this can get distorted through imbalanced teaching. What if we create a culture of compulsory ecstasy despite painful situations because "Jesus loves us"? What if you're not grinning like you've got a coat hanger in your mouth – does this mean you're not walking close to God? What if people feel pressured to do spiritual cartwheels for fear of being judged for being real?

I think God wants us to be exactly that – real, with Him and ourselves, and Scripture gives us countless examples of people who did just that. You've only got to skim over the Psalms to see this sort of faith in action.

Sometimes our understanding of the gospel (or lack of it) can let us down. Because of Jesus we don't have to strive to earn God's love like a Scout earns his badges. Thankfully, we're not judged on our performance but His.

We don't have to be Superman because He already is. This truth remains if we're doing backflips on mountaintops or curling into the foetal position.

The burned-out elephant in the room...

You may have noticed that burnout is not an easy subject to talk about. You'd think it would be easier in the context of Christian ministry, but often I think that, actually, it makes it harder still.

Burnout can be a little bit like an elephant in the room. Something that's blatantly in front of you but maybe you react to the elephant's trunk like an ostrich with its head in the sand.

It's so important we're real with each other and ourselves. When I was too stricken by grief to even see it, Cath pointed the elephant out to me, close friends were concerned for me, and my pastor gently prodded me.

After getting the sick note, I was off work probably for about six weeks, with another few weeks phasing back into work. For many, it can be much worse and the recovery time would need to be much longer.

The root of my burnout was pretty obvious. Though I had great support, I walked through losing my dad at a young age and held the weight of "next of kin" on my shoulders. Somewhere along the way I buckled under the ever-mounting weight as it exceeded my capacity.

But sometimes the root can be a little less obvious, the symptoms played down, the signals harder to spot, and the diagnosis tougher to accept. But I think it's important to not be ostriches to elephants. To not bury our heads in the sand rather than face reality. Why? Because I believe that health matters and the alternative is far worse.

Owning the irony of brokenness

There's a well-known phrase that goes "what doesn't kill you makes you stronger". For me, having gone through grief and burnout, I bear the battle scars from the fight, but they have faded and for the most part are not that visible. Remember when Jacob wrestled with God? He had his hip dislocated – he came out the other side with a new identity, but from that moment onwards he walked with a limp.

I think burnout leaves you with such a limp. And perhaps on the surface it looks like a weakness, but my small contribution to this discussion is, like the phrase suggests, actually I think it makes you stronger. Speaking personally, I've had a heightened understanding that I can't do everything. I have limits. I have a deeper realization that I need God instead of taking on the world for God and forgetting to let Him help me do it.

My limp humbles me, it reminds me I'm broken and in need of fixing. It keeps me thankful as I refocus on the promise that Jesus makes me whole, and then I rejoice that I not only get to experience this in part now, but that I'll know it fully when He returns.

My limp also helps me connect with people who have suffered in a way that I couldn't have before. How do we reach a broken world with God's love? I think it's by "limpers" not pretending to be Olympic sprinters. It's by broken people pointing to a fixing God. It's by having your brokenness on display rather than covering it up, owning it instead of being in denial of it. Not as a badge of honour where your grief gives you a sense of entitlement, but wearing it all the same. The more you wear it, the more comfortable it gets and the more other badge-wearers see it on you too.

DAI DICTIONARY

Zip, Zap, Boing – three years studying Drama at Uni and this game is what I remember.

PRAYER

Lord.
Make a note that I have a sick note.
It doesn't give me my identity but it gives me space to find it.
Thank You that I don't have to be a hero.
Thank You that I don't have to fly,
have laser beams for eyes,
or smash people when I get big, green, and angry (that would be fun with some people though)

Thank You that I can just be.
In the thickness of my sickness
You carry and sustain me.

Thank You that You put back together exploding thermometers.
Help me to not vacate myself from being in Your hands
Help me to not be that ostrich with his head buried in the sand
Thank You that no matter how big my burnout elephant is
You're bigger.
And in Your strength – I'm going to get better.

RE: PRAYER

Come to Me.
Know that I'm not judging you with performance marks
out of 10.
Know that it's OK to have a limp (*can I get an Amen*?)

Come to Me.
If you want to be like Me
If you want to reflect Me
Be you (not fake you, but real you)
Just don't do it without Me.

I don't need your masks,
Or your buried heads
I just want you near Me
because that's when you get fed.

If you're burned out – come to Me
If life gives you a knockout
If you're out for the count or in a drought – come to Me

If you're stuck in a rut
If your coping door
Or opportunity window is shut
If the pressure's just too much – come to Me.

Just come
And be.

"Come to me, all who labour and are heavy laden, and I will give you rest. Take my yoke upon you, and learn from me, for I am gentle and lowly in heart, and you will find rest for your souls. For my yoke is easy, and my burden is light."

Matthew 11:28–30

LORD
THE PACE OF THE
RACE
IS MOVING AT
AN INCREDIBLE
PACE
THE G-FORCE
IS PULLING
FUNNY LOOKS
ON MY FACE

Chapter 9

IT'S ALL CHANGE

Dad shaped holes

Doing life without Dad is a bit like having a full English without the hash browns. You can still enjoy it, but you just know something's missing.

You've probably heard the saying "life goes on", but for me it goes on with a Dad shaped hole (a slender 5 ft 11 hole with a piratesque earring on the left ear).

Dad shaped holes
With parakeet shoulder perching birds.

Dad shaped holes
In rock songs booming through speaker cones.

I see Dad shaped holes
Every time there's a moment to quote Blackadder and he's not there to take part.

I feel Dad shaped holes
When I'm in the car and I'm only in the mood for a Dad shaped phone call.

I hear Dad shaped holes
In the occasional silences that are left behind in family gatherings, which would have usually been taken up by Dad doing or saying something funny yet left field.

I hear **Dad shaped holes**
When I just feel like listening to his stories.

I hear **Dad shaped holes**
When I hear Bob Dylan remind us that times change,
followed by the harmonica bit of course.

I see **Dad shaped holes**
In soldiers standing tall
In boot camp reality programmes on TV catch-up
platforms

I hear **Dad shaped holes**
Whenever someone talks without stopping for air.

There are **Dad shaped holes**
When I see slightly pronounced eyebrows.

I hear whispers of **Dad shaped holes**
When I see Bear Grylls* sink his teeth into something
which you won't find on a Michelin-starred* menu, like
a bullfrog's spleen or an anaconda's appendix.

I hear **Dad shaped holes**
Every time I hear a motorbike revving, sounding
reverberation through the exhaust.

I feel **Dad shaped holes**
In Jim Carrey movie roles
from the nineties and noughties

And there are **Dad shaped holes** in my car moments.
I especially miss sharing car moments with him.

Car moments

JOURNAL

30 October 2015

It's funny how grief comes and goes. It's like a queue at Starbucks just before rush hour. Today has been a day when I've remembered Dad. It has felt magical to remember my old man, yet it's still tainted with such deep sadness that he is no longer here.

What I find hard as I continue to reflect is the fact that everything has changed so much in such a short space of time. In the last two and a half years since Dad passed – I've had three birthdays, the middle one of those entering a new decade of my life. I've moved house and become a homeowner. I've changed jobs, changed cars three times, twice become an award-winning spoken-word artist, dedicated a video on remembrance to Dad, gotten two tattoos in tribute to my two Fathers (heavenly and earthly), and have been asked to write a book on grief.

For me, it's the little things where I most remember Dad. I write this entry suddenly because just yesterday I bought a Honda Civic. I wish I could share this moment with him. I wish I could share that I too have become/am becoming a lover of the Honda. It's stupid I know – he just enjoyed cars and as he understood little of what I did for a living, it would have been something we could've enjoyed together.

I guess we have a relationship with cars, Dad and I, which goes back years. He used to take me to industrial estates just to shout at me, or that's what it felt like sometimes. It was never aggressive, just comic gold stuff as he flinched and pounced at me stalling, kangaroo jumps, and impending contacts with stationary vehicles. Not just cars, mind, but bikes too. I remember hanging on the back of Dad's bike as we glided through the Welsh countryside on his 20-plus-year-old BMW boxer engine.

Dad also taught me how to bump-start a car. When my car was flat up Bewts mountain... (a place that, when the sun sets, gives the darkest of black holes a run for its money). I remember Cath and I had been having a big heart-to-heart with the engine off and all the lights on... Two hours later, and it had as much chance of starting as I do getting out of bed at 5 a.m. in the morning. I tried pushing the car but it was stuck – the tyres had found a nice little groove in the gravel of some car park. Cath's efforts of pushing were, how can I put it... Well, she gets points for trying. At the time I was driving a Ford Ka, given to me by Dad. I managed to lift it, give it a shove, and hey presto, it was moving.

Wait a minute – it's moving.

It's pitch black in the middle of nowhere and Cath and I are watching our only mode of transport going rogue and taking a stroll through the finest countryside Wales has to offer. I start pegging it towards the car, catch up with it, slip into the driver's seat, and turn it back onto the road just before it heads off into a ravine. (Alright, maybe it was just a hedge or some brambles, but at the time I felt like a cross between Rambo* and the Stig.*) So, the car is off the gravel car park, I'm in it – but it's still flat. That's when I give my dad a call.

"Dad, do you know how to bump-start a car?"

"You'll need to give it a push."

Done that, I'm thinking as I'm wiping the sweat off my brow.

"You need to pick up speed."

That won't be a problem, I'm thinking as I now find myself on what must've been a 10 per cent gradient at the top of a mountain.

"Let it free run and then put it into second."

"Alright, I'll do it now." Dad stays on the phone.

"No luck Dad."

"Oh."

"Oh hang on... do I need to turn the ignition?"

"Yes!"

I try it again... handbrake down as I let it free run down the mountain away from Cath... If I had been able to see her blonde bob go further into the distance in my rear-view mirror I'm sure it would've been pretty funny, but I couldn't – did I mention it was pitch black?

So now I'm in the car, picking up speed and free falling (I'm a sucker for stuff that's free, even if it is falling).

Now or never, I'm thinking... *alright just a couple more seconds, then clutch down into second, and... hey presto.* All of a sudden I feel like David Blaine* or Dynamo* after a big magic trick; it actually worked!! I put my lights on and then not ten seconds later a boy racer comes hurtling up the mountain, passing me by a couple of whiskers. Seconds later... we would've crashed head-on for sure.

Cath runs down to meet me, calls me her hero, and there goes a memorable evening.

Like I said, car memories are fun. I've since had a few more but that's a story for another day (or a chapter for another book).

The big move

Barely seven months after the funeral, Cath and I moved house. But this was more exciting than just any standard box, tape, and all hands on deck move because in October 2013 we moved into our first house. I'm not saying we lived in garages or chicken coops up until that point, we lived in houses before too, it's just that this time the keys opened the door to us becoming homeowners. It was a great move. Family and friends showed up with vans, anti-bac spray, and elbow grease.

Two months on again and I started a new job. After seven years working for a Christian charity called Going Public, I began working for the Bible Society. At the time, Cath and I were also exploring church in our local community and everything that came with it. So much change, so many new things – and knowing that Dad wouldn't get to see these changes was a hard reality to stomach.

One of the hardest parts of the grief experience for me is that life continues and moves forward, but Dad no longer gets to be a part of it. He will forever be engrained in our memories but until we meet again, that's the only place where he lives, a collection of memories, some amazing, some painful. No longer does he reside in the active moments, but the past moments – he now lives in the memory.

Looking back, I can see that things were moving at a phenomenal speed. The sense of perspective on life had broadened so much for me that big decisions seemed smaller in the context of life or death. It got a bit addictive at one stage; I felt a freedom in change and moving forward, probably because it gave me a sense of progress... one which seemed way off in my grief. Some changes were just what I needed; other bits needed the brakes to be put on as the timing just wasn't right. With help, Cath and I realized we had to adopt a slower pace to life, a jog instead of a sprint (or maybe one of those funny shuffles you see race walkers* do). Still, some were big steps and others were smaller. Either way, grief taught me the art of one step at a time, even if I do need to relearn it once in a while.

DAI DICTIONARY

Bear Grylls – an army man turned survival expert who loves Jesus. A top-notch guy who you shouldn't play truth or dare with.

Michelin – no not the tyres, the fancy food reviewers (like TripAdvisor but proper official like).

Rambo – Sylvester Stallone when he wasn't crying "Adrian" with boxing gloves.

Stig – we've covered this guy in chapter 4.

David Blaine – don't offer him ice 'cos it will remind him of that time he got frozen in time... (Square).

Dynamo – now you see him, now you... wait where's he gone?

Race walking – like this guy (to be fair I walk a bit like this at normal speed):
https://www.youtube.com/watch?v=2urNVmKnEaQ

PRAYER

Lord
The pace of the race is
Moving at an incredible pace
The G force is pulling funny looks on my face.

Lots of changes
And they feel all at once
Rather than stages.

It feels good but it feels too fast
It feels empty with the man who played my Dad
No longer on the cast.

I see Dad shaped holes
Everywhere I go

A feeling
    Of seeming
        Content in the direction my life is moving
            But it hurts
                Because it's moving without him.

RE: PRAYER

Know that when all seems like it's changing
Know that I don't change
Because I AM the unchanging

I'm your bedrock when the earth plates beneath your
feet are moving
Remember – life is like faith
It's a marathon not a sprint
And remember, every step of the way
I'm with you in it.

"Brothers, I do not consider that I have made it my own. But one thing I do: forgetting what lies behind and straining forward to what lies ahead, I press on towards the goal for the prize of the upward call of God in Christ Jesus."

Philippians 3:13–14

HEALING MOMENTS
DAD DISPLAY
TABLET TAKING
POOL POTTING
LIONS LIKING
CHAIR CHATTING
ITCHING FOR AN INKING
VIVID VISITS
SCRIPTURE SINKING
REMEMBRANCE
REMEMBERING

Chapter
10

HEALING MOMENTS

The beauty contest

One of my proudest moments in life had to be when I came first in a beauty competition. I'd like to say I can remember it like it was yesterday but then I'd have to repent for lying through my gums. I don't remember it, of course I don't, I was one. But when I was old enough to remember, my mam* would tell me of this amazing achievement and I must confess, it was a good feeling. I wouldn't go as far as to say that it was the bedrock on which I built my self-image identity but it did make me feel good about myself. Years later (and I mean years – I was about sixteen), I stumbled upon further evidence from that contest which was held in the hub of a small caravan holiday park down in south west Wales. The reason I won was because there wasn't much competition, well actually there wasn't any; I was the only beauty baby in my category. It wasn't down to my squeezy cheeks, sailor's outfit, how I held my rusk,* or even how much I dribbled; I was the prizewinner because my birth certificate said so. My whole life had been a lie... well, the contest was at least.

That's a memory that still makes me smirk now, when occasionally it comes up in conversation and my mam holds fast that I would have won regardless of the number of participants (#obvs!), though I guess that's one of life's big mysteries that won't be solved until we get to heaven.

The scream, the sink, and the stumble

Another memory that Mam occasionally refers to is yet another time when I was in nappies. We were in a café and a waitress was bringing a pot of tea to the table. I'm not sure what happened, she must have slipped or fumbled the tray, but the tea escaped from inside the pot and ended up on me – all over me. It all happened so fast. And it doesn't matter if it's infused with Tetley's best or not, boiling water is boiling water and I screeched and screamed with my little lungs at maximum capacity. If you knew my mam, you would know that she is one of the kindest and most caring people you will ever meet. She's strong-willed and determined but can be quite timid too. Hers is a soft, gentle voice which goes higher in pitch rather than volume when she's calling you from a distance. She certainly doesn't throw her weight around or make demands and she's not one to put people out or make a fuss. Well, a mother's nature overrides the need to meet social etiquette. Mam recalls how she barged her way past the waitress (who to be fair felt terrible) and stormed straight into the kitchen of this old-school caff. She plunged me into the sink and put the cold tap on full. While all this was happening I continued to screech and scream. Mam may come across as timid but she's a sharp cookie (and formerly a nurse). She reacted fast and because of her quick thinking, thirty years on I don't have scars from third-degree burns – that splurge of instant cold water was a healing moment.

In this chapter I want to address those moments in grief where you start to see light breaking through at the end of the tunnel. Often we can't see the light when we're in the tunnel, but that's not because it's not there. Rather, it's because we're not far enough along to see the light at the other end. I want to share with you some of my light-breaking "healing moments". This is by no means a one size fits all list; some may be similar to others' grieving, but some will be completely different because they are personal. Either way, allow me to offer some of mine.

My healing moments

As a communicator I quite like to talk. And as Dad was taken from us all too soon, I felt that I had more to say. The best way through my grief was to process it, to actively pursue a conversation I wasn't ready to finish.

1. The grief gallery/the Dad display

Early on in my grief, when I was given time off work by the doctor, I spent the first week creating a gallery to honour my dad. There was a picture of Dad barely twenty years old and on duty in Northern Ireland, there was another of Dad in his Welsh Guards glad rags, there was a medal which he received from his service, there was a beret, and there was a picture of me and Dad together in the most recent photo I could find.

I bought photo frames of varying sizes, I went on eBay and bid for medal frames and beret frames. I took out the display prints and replaced them with Dad prints. I carefully Blu-tack'ed them to the border so they'd sit neatly in the centre of the frame. At the back of the frame I screwed in screw hooks and tied string to them so the pictures could rest on picture hooks. After that, I laid them all out on the sanded wooden floor of our living room, and figured out the most symmetrical way that these memories could be displayed. I marked the same distance between each memory with a pen and a measuring tape. Then I lifted them from the floor to the wall. And so as I entered that house through the front door, I only had to look to the left to see Dad on display. Most nights after I brushed my teeth, I'd walk down the hallway to the front door and salute my late father with minty fresh breath. In the midst of my stomach-turning turmoil it would give me a sense of peace. It was a way for me to continue the conversation that was cut so short.

2. Tablet taking

I've covered this already but I felt it appropriate to put here because it was a healing moment for me. No pill is an answer to all our problems, but if they can help and not hinder, if they give you that little extra strength to keep going on the journey, maybe they're worth it. I've already told you my story and I invite you to prayerfully consider what's best for you.

3. Pool potting...

In my heyday I wasn't too shabby at pool. It was a bonding ritual I shared with my old man from the age of about twelve. He bought me a "Jimmy White* Pool Master" from the local sports shop and we'd walk up the road to our local pub and hit a few balls. I started by miscuing balls, then worked my way up to hitting them (not in the aggressive sense of course), but sooner or later I was potting them. My finest moment (which Dad often retold) was when I beat the under-16 Wales champion at the age of fourteen, but that wasn't such a daunting task at the time because I thought I'd already beaten him (Dad thought he was a different bloke). But still, eventually I had beaten both the genuine pool whiz and the imposter. I was in my prime when I was fourteen, when I had the stature of a miniature garden rake. We'd buy in some nuts, Dad would have a beer and I a coke. And then we'd play for hours as Dad would put "Kayleigh – Didn't You Know You Broke My Heart" on the jukebox and sing along with out-of-tune gusto. (If you want to get a taste, look it up on YouTube.)

So having said goodbye to Dad before I was ready, pool became another conversation with him, another way to connect with a man I was grieving for. And so I'd go down the local pool hall with a few of the boys, Ads, Jonny, Steve, and Ruben to name a few. I even won a Jimmy White Pool Master on eBay and started potting again, even if Ads did usually beat me (like I said, fourteen was when I was in my prime).

4. Lions liking/rugby roaring

During the first few months of my grief, having any creative connection with God was too tough a door to prise open. Before, my faith was the only thing I'd be really interested in engaging with to get my creative writing juices pulsing. But after it hit the fan, it became too painful for me to write/create and so I stopped for a bit. In the summer of 2013, a few months after Dad passed, the British and Irish Lions* were playing a series Down Under and it was a great form of escapism for me. I upgraded my Sky package (for one month only, I'm not made of money!) and invited the crème de la crème of British athletes into my living room as I egged them on in every match. I also wrote a spoken word piece prophesying the victory of the Lion over the Wallaby... and it was fulfilled!

It may sound naff to you (especially if you're not a

fan of rugby), but to me it was spiritual. It was a form of escapism that massaged my irregular beating heart and, having taken a breather from faith poetry, I picked up my pen again and began writing rhymes on rugby. Even if it was just about the oval-shaped ball... it was key in welcoming me back into writing and it wasn't much longer after that when I started connecting my creativity back to my creator again. I just needed a bit of space to find my way back, and the breadcrumbs along the path were George North, Johnny Sexton, and Manu Tuliagi. You can see the result here: www.youtube.com/watch?v=uG2V2aJ9PsA

5. Chair chatting

I wouldn't typically recommend pool halls and rugby blogging to everyone as a means of coping with grief, but this one in my view is a no-brainer. The leadership team at my church, Glenwood asked whether counselling would be something I'd consider and generously offered to cover the cost of the first few sessions. It was a little bit of a slow start for me but the more I went, the more I looked forward to going. I really connected with the counsellor, who shared my faith and listened to my sentences. Sometimes I was intense, other times light-hearted, sometimes we laughed, other times I choked up and had to take an intake of breath before finishing my train of thought. What I do know is that a fifty-minute session every two weeks was a huge blessing to me, with doses of revelation. I met with Ann probably over a period of about six months, and it was uplifting to look back on the journey and visibly see the strides that we made. Ann was fantastic. She listened, she engaged in conversation and was like a dance partner, she was there every step of the way but also let me take the lead.

6. An itching for an inking

You may remember me mentioning that Dad had ink. He used to joke and encourage me to join him in the tattoo department but it was something I was pretty indifferent about when I was younger. For starters it's permanent. Secondly, his choice of having a panther getting strangled by a cobra as a forearm display wasn't a case-winning convincer either. In my twenties I flirted with the idea of having some "Christian" ink, I liked the idea of feeling holy on the one hand and "edgy" on the other. I'm glad I didn't at that time because it wouldn't have been for the right reasons, but as I was grieving Dad this became another way to continue the dialogue, to pay tribute to a man who was no longer with us, to say "I remember". And so with that in mind – I have a poppy on my ankle to "remember" my old man and a cross on my forearm to remind me that my eternal destiny has changed because of Jesus.

There may be different views on this from a biblical perspective, but for me it was the right decision all day long. Why? Because it reconnects me to Jesus and reconnects me to Dad.

7. Vivid crem visits

As I've explained before, this is not a fun day out, but nevertheless it's still part of the healing process. We've got a little routine going on Dad occasions. We visit the crem, pop some flowers in the memorial pot, spot the horses in the opposite field, take a picture, go for lunch close by, and simply remember. Every time it gets that bit easier and that bit more special.

Mam, Dylan my brother, and my sister Jess, all came with me to visit Dad's tree to celebrate Father's Day just a few days before me writing this. The tree had looked pretty sorry for itself the past few times we'd been down but the other day it had grown, had a full spread of leaves, and a chunky trunk. It brought a lightness to my spirit and a wry smile to my face that I wasn't expecting (just like when I wrote the word "chunky" – can't help but think of the hippo in *Madagascar**).

8. Scripture sinking

I'm not going to pretend that I turned to God's word as much as I would have liked, but the moments I did, where Scripture spoke to me or was spoken over me, were massive, in prayer or on cards. John 11:35 will forever speak to me of the Father heart of God because we see the Father by looking to the Son. How did Jesus respond to suffering and grief? He broke down and wept.

9. Remembering the remembrance

In November 2014 we celebrated the centenary of World War I. It was also roughly 18 months on from me saying goodbye to Dad. I wanted to remember a man who fought in conflict and similarly address the issue of suffering from a biblical perspective. What is God's take on death and suffering? The only way I knew how, was to humbly speak one verse repeatedly. The shortest verse in Scripture, the one I just mentioned: John 11:35. We shot it in one take with the Cenotaph in Whitehall, London, as our backdrop.

Usually I use actors for shooting footage that complements the spoken word piece, but it was crucial to me that every part of this was authentic. And so when I referenced soldiers, we shot scenes of a church planter who used to be a marine. When I referenced those who suffered, I held Dad's service medal and Rachel took a flower to the grave of her late husband (she now has three gorgeous boys and another husband, my best pal – Ads, the guy who terrorized my letterbox at two in the morning, remember?). This video was a big deal to me and I'm thankful to those who helped me do it. I felt the need to be a voice for those who suffer and to speak hope to those who had possibly lost it. How? By pointing to the tears of Jesus in God's word. To remind people that when we weep, we don't weep alone, because He weeps with us. You can see the film at http://spoken-truth.com/john1135.

Now and not yet

As I conclude this chapter, I want to encourage you to recognize that there is light at the end of the tunnel, even if all you see is darkness, even if all you see is the absence of light – know it's there. For me, the moments I've reflected on in this chapter were healing moments. Some big, some small – but all significant in my journey to being restored. I encourage you, if you're struggling through grief right now, to consider what those healing moments could be in your life, however trivial they may seem on the surface.

I also recognize that I'm not the finished article yet. I've come a long way in these three or so years but I also know that after this experience I will never be the same. As I'm writing this, I still haven't mustered up the strength to put Dad's display back up since we moved house in October 2013. Not just that, but my recent trip to the crem on Father's Day was a mere five days ago and it was too tough to buy the flowers to place under Dad's tree. I know that grief has reshaped and remoulded me. I know that my heart has healed from much, but I also know that this healing will be an ongoing process. I know that I'll only get the answers to some questions when I eventually arrive at my heavenly home. I know that I may not be fully restored until I get there. And I know that this is OK because it's a snapshot of a bigger picture, the now and not yet kingdom of God restoring brokenness. I get to experience the beauty of restoration and simultaneously hope for the ultimate restoration when Christ returns in all His splendour.

DAI DICTIONARY

Rusks – I don't know, are they like biscuits for babies? You probably sank your gums into these bad boys yourself.

Jimmy White – a dab hand at snooker who never won the world title.

The Lions – best of the best from the UK join forces to take on the Southern Hemisphere at rugby.

Madagascar – remember Ross from Friends? Well, turns out he's a talking lion and his best friend is a stripy Chris Rock.

PRAYER

Thank You for healing moments
For my
Pool potting
and
Vivid visits

Thank You for
The rugby roaring
Chair chatting
Gallery Grieving moments

Thank You for Your healing moments
For the
Light breaking
Hope making
moments
To the tunnel travellers.

Doses of revelation
and maybe even medication.
Crem visits and pain threshold limits
With tattoo exhibits
That help me
Remember and
yet still surrender.

To the one who knows
To the one in us who flows
To the one in whom we grow.
To the one we know
For the one we call ourselves "known"

RE: PRAYER

You've said it right
At the end of the tunnel, there is light.
How do I know?
I am the light of the world.
And I came to restore a broken world.

Know that the healing of the world is in operation.
Turn to Me and know I'll give you restoration.
Know that I'm gleaming
In every moment of your healing.

Know that I'm cleaning –

And know that when you confess
That I'm there to clean up the mess
The broken bits
The bits that hurt

"But he was pierced for our transgressions; he was crushed for our iniquities; upon him was the chastisement that brought us peace, and with his wounds we are healed."

Isaiah 53:5

THERE'S NOT LONG LEFT
THERE'S MORE
AND MORE GAPS
BETWEEN THE
IN AND OUT BREATHS
HAVE FAITH
BECAUSE WHEN FAITH IS
FOUND IN ME
YOU GO STRAIGHT
FROM PASSING
INTO THE ARMS OF THE
EVERLASTING

Chapter
11

FAITH IN FAITH

There's an eclectic collection of memories that spring to mind when I reflect on my father and his journey with faith. In this chapter I'm flicking through the memory books, searching for the moments that Dad engaged with all things God, church, and the faith of following Jesus.

Dad's faith was complicated. Not that any faith is ever really that straightforward, black and white, or a perfect circle (we do love a good circle, don't we?). I'm going to take a punt and say most people's faith journey as followers of Jesus is a bit of a paradox – one that can be consistently complex yet perfectly simple; I know mine is. I'm a Christian, not because of what I contribute but because of what Christ conquered.

That said, Dad had a complex faith. If someone were to ask me if Dad was a Christian, I'd hesitate before giving an answer. Why? Because for me it was never a simple yes or no on the ballot paper answer. Over the years we probably spent days doing "faith conversations". Talking about faith, prayer, where God is in the suffering and the bits in between. As Dad was a bit of a talker we'd go round the mulberry bush a bit and take a few tangential detours on the way, but talking God stuff with my old man was, simply put, quality. Sometimes we'd chat about Jesus' divinity in the one breath, with something Dad said to someone about something totally different thirty years ago in the next. Sticking to point would sometimes be challenging, but it would always be a fun way of doing God and life chats. Dad was a bit of a storyteller when he got going and I reckon the ultimate storyteller enjoyed it as much as we did.

"I pray every night Dave..."
Is what Dad used to say.

"I
Pray
Every
Night."

And I know he did. After he settled for bed, before he'd go to sleep he'd say a short prayer. Something like...

"Dear God
Please look after David, Cath, Dylan, and Jessica. Amen."

He'd pray that God would keep us safe.
   Wow.
   Pause button.
   Dad patrolled the unsettled streets of Northern Ireland and he mined down in seams shorter than a grasshopper's kneecap.* Dad spent years of his life holding down some of the most dangerous jobs going and he tells me that every night before bed, he'd pray that *we* were safe.
   To my knowledge, my old man didn't go on long prayer walks, he didn't write down words of encouragement in

a journal, and the only reason he fasted Facebook was because he had no idea how to use it. And although these are all good, even godly, things to do, things that help us connect with God more profoundly – I don't think God sees them as salvation deal-breakers.

The best example of a Christian I know...

That's what Dad used to say about me. I'm not adding that in to brag. I'm the first to say that actually I'm not that perfect (and I'm sure Cath would give an Amen somewhere in this sentence too). I have lots of flaws: as a reflector I am quite capable of being self-absorbed, I can get grumpy and envious, I like being right even when I'm not, and I can easily get lazy with my faith, to name a few right off the bat. And the list doesn't stop there, but Dad saying that he thought I was one of the best examples of a Christian he knew meant so much because, unsurprisingly, he knew me. He knew my heart, he had a handle on my lifestyle, and as an observant man, he was probably taking note of what I did and said even when I wasn't.

It makes me think, as a Christian we're witnesses even when we're not witness to it. I mean how we act when someone cuts us up on the motorway, how we speak about people when they're not in earshot, when we speak up and when we bite our lip – if you're a Christian, it all counts because we're representing Jesus even when we don't realize it.

The Gospel according to Samuel L. Jackson

Ger would quote Scripture to me, but it wouldn't be the classics like John 3:16 or 1 Corinthians 13; he'd remind me that Jesus turned water into wine or quote from the epically cool Samuel L. in *Pulp Fiction*.

Samuel L. Jackson's character is a gangster who was cooked up by Tarantino... There's this one scene where he's all suited and booted, black suit, white shirt, and tie, and with criminal colleague, T-bird Travolta, he pays a couple of guys a visit. He starts off talking about the tastiness of the Kahuna burger from that Hawaii joint the other side of town and then with mad eyes and a big Afro he recites Ezekiel 25:17 and then proceeds to "pop a cap" in someone's American-coined donkey (you know, shoot someone).

There would always be a wry smile whenever Dad would quote it, it was tongue in cheek, but I can see why this was one of Dad's favourite "passages of Scripture". It's a no-messing monologue typed by Tarantino and executed epically by Samuel L. Jackson, even if it is a dangerous verse to take out of context and a misquote of what it actually says.

Hand-raising Christians

I don't know how or if you express your feelings, but many Christians express their gratitude to God through collective song. We call it worship and people express this gratitude in different ways. Some people dance, some people wave flags well, others just wave flags, some people sway, some people sit, some people rustle change with their hands in their pockets, while some people just kneel. Some other people raise their hands in worship. I don't think there's a points system of certain moves you need to get into your worship routine and I don't think God gives us difficulty or execution scores. We all express ourselves in different ways and the most important thing, in my view, is that we express our gratitude to God, however that looks. And that's coming from a swaying, sitting hand-raiser (though not usually at the same time).

I remember Dad telling me he didn't get why people raised their hands in church, he thought it was disrespectful. His experience of church was going on a Sunday as a kid because that's just what you did. The songs he sang were hymns (which is not a bad thing by any means, he just wasn't used to thirty-minute blocks of worship with Worship Central* choruses). Any mention of God was done with such utter reverence that if you broke a smile you'd probably feel like you'd sinned, and so you can understand why he thought any sort of hand motions would be disrespectful. Yet, as I used to raise my hands during the penultimate verse of *In Christ Alone** I'd try and defend the action. It's a funny one, thinking about it. The whole of Wales (me included) would erupt in air-punching thanksgiving whenever Shane Williams* (or Phil Bennett*) did a sidestep on the rugby pitch, but if you raise your hand to the King of kings in a church building – you can be labelled an eccentric.

Religion doesn't do itself any favours...

As I reflect on Dad's attitude to religion and why he wasn't a big fan of church, it doesn't take long to come up with some reasons why.

As I said, my old man went along to chapel as a kid, probably begrudgingly and maybe that was a factor in why he never really connected with it. Then, as soon as he could pick up a razor he was also picking up assault rifles as he trained with the Welsh Guards regiment of the army. Not long after that he was serving in Northern Ireland, seeing first-hand what was done in the name of religion and politics, with car bombs and violence a regular occurrence.

He lost friends in conflicts and spent lots of his life battling with the after-effects of what he experienced. I don't think he ever really knew how much God loved him, but then do any of us? But as he journeyed through life, up cropped more questions such as "Where was God when I needed Him?" than a knowingness of God's closeness. I could point him to some verses which would speak about the love of God, but I must confess they were not easy questions to answer. I hadn't seen what Dad had seen, I hadn't experienced war at first-hand, I hadn't been thrown off my feet in a car explosion or borne the responsibility of being so skint during the miners' strike that I literally didn't know where the next meal was coming from.

Dad's experience of religion was tarnished at best, and the truth is, sometimes religion doesn't do itself any favours. Sometimes church isn't a helpful picture of the love of God and sometimes people who wear the name badge "Christian" act in ways that couldn't be further from Jesus if they tried.

Faith on the deathbed...

Like I alluded to earlier, I wouldn't shout from the rooftops that Dad was a Christian because the truth is I didn't really know either way, but those last four days he had on this earth were fleeting yet so, so important.

I remember a couple of days into that time, a church leader and good friend of mine came down from Cardiff to show his support and pray. We were feeling pretty flat at the time, having just spent the last two days seeing Dad go from looking in a bad way to looking even worse. Seeing Dad deteriorate right in front of me was certainly taking its toll. Norman came in and introduced himself to Dad, who was semi-conscious through the cocktail of sheer pain and pain relief. He prayed for Dad, spoke a blessing over him, and then anointed his head with oil. What happened next was amazing; from nowhere Dad almost found a new lease of life as he engaged with it all. For any cynics out there I know a big factor was the oil; as it slowly travelled down Dad's forehead you could see Dad connect with the texture – the smell, the warmth – but it was more than just a trigger of the senses, it was a God moment. And the blessings and the prayers were just as much a part of it.

Over the course of Dad's decline, we had more God moments.

We prayed, Cath sang some of his favourite Welsh hymns over him, and I recited a poem I'd written called "Counting Down the Hours". I guess it was less a poem and more a promise with echoes of Revelation's no more pain and tears on the other side.

We talked.

I prayed.

Mam prayed.

Cath prayed.

He could barely move, but even at the end there were moments where Dad's eyes said so much. As he finally let go we assured him that there was a loving heavenly Father waiting for him on the other side.

Like I said earlier, Dad's faith was complex. It wasn't anchored in the knowledge that he was loved unconditionally; it wasn't fastened together with the reality that Jesus' sacrifice on a tree up some hill 2,000 years ago was personally for him. I know Dad experienced good bits that link to Jesus, the church, and the Christian faith. I'm blessed and humbled to even think I had a small part to play in it. But I also know Dad experienced his fair share of suffering, which brought about the response,

> *"if God's up there, then*
> *tell Him to*
> *give me a break,*
> *tell Him to*
> *cut me some slack."*

It may seem crazy to you, but I know that in those final moments Dad had a God moment. How? Because I had it too. So did Cath. So did Mam. It was a tear-filled, heartbreaking fellowship of church by a hospital bed that was soon to become a deathbed.

So now if someone asks me if Dad was a Christian, I hesitate. But the hesitation's different; I don't wrestle with the complexities of Dad's faith journey or the ifs of repentance or the evidence of a commitment. I hesitate because I take a moment to remember *that* God moment and then I respond, "Yeah... yeah he was".

Can I be sure, 100 per cent?

No.

But I truly believe Dad accepted Jesus before he passed.

I choose to have faith in the fact that Dad had faith.

But more than that – my faith is not just in a human response, it's in a God whose love is total, whose pursuit of seekers is unceasing. My faith is in a God who laid down everything to give us the opportunity to be in relationship with Him. And as I witnessed Dad searching in those final moments, I have no doubt in my mind – not that Dad found God, but that Dad was found by God. And in this I have a peace that passes understanding.

DAI DICTIONARY

Grasshopper's kneecap – just my take on the well-known phrase.

Worship Central – Tim Hughes and all those boys. They're good, mind, but I'll have it known I prefer Sound of Wales, and no, that's got absolutely nothing to do with the fact that I'm married to the worship leader... How dare you, well I'm really disappointed.

In Christ Alone – one of the greatest modern hymns full stop. By Stuart Townend. (By the way, the hand-raising bit I'm referring to is "and as he STANDS in victory".)

Shane Williams – a 5 ft something Welsh rugby winger from the Amman Valley (Cath's sister used to be in his class at school!).

Phil Bennett – is what you get when you cross sidesteps with jawlines.

PRAYER

Lord.
        Take him home.

There's not long left
There's more and more gaps between the in and out
breaths.

The spark's fading
The life in eyes is dimming
The fire's going out.

What I see in front of me
Is a not long left reality
The soon to be passing finality

Lord
        Take him home.

And give me peace and clarity
That he's arrived there home safely
Burden, pain, and affliction free
Home
In the embrace
Of the giver of grace.

In Your arms
        May he know

RE: PRAYER

I know you can't see round the other side of passing
But have faith
Because when faith is found in Me
You go straight from passing into the arms of the
everlasting.

A place where you're met with a joy surpassing
Any other joy you previously basked in.

Your life on earth was never the final destination
    The end goal is constant company
        with Me
            Creator of Creation.

"Behold, I stand at the door and knock. If anyone hears my voice and opens the door, I will come in to him and eat with him, and he with me."

Revelation 3:20

"Truly, I say to you, today you will be with me in paradise."

Luke 23:43

Counting down the hours

A poem

"Looking forward, but not losing sight"

https://youtu.be/jQQZ18BS1gc

GOD
I ASK HUMBLY
IF YOU WOULD HEAL ME
HEAL ME WHEN I
HYPERVENTILATE
HEAL ME WHEN I
GET IN A PANICKED STATE
MAY YOU COME TO ME
WITH ALL YOUR FEARS AND KNOW
ONE DAY
I'LL WIPE
AWAY YOUR
TEARS

Chapter
12

THE "H" WORD

If you're a Christian and you take the Bible as God's word, you'd be hard pressed to argue that God didn't heal and do miracles. Just look at Jesus and what He did in the Gospels. He changed molecular structures – He went for a wander on the water, He shushed a storm into silence (and threatened the naughty step), He made bloomer loaves multiply through prayer, He turned groggy bathwater into vintage wine, He told a paraplegic to pick up his mat and start walking, He even gave a blind man the ability to read the really, really small letters at the optician's, no glasses needed! That's a handful of the stuff that we read about in the Gospels and at the end of John's Gospel, John even goes on to say that the stuff he wrote was just a snapshot of what Jesus did.

A few years back I remember hearing a story of someone who was miraculously healed. It was in this church about an hour's drive from my place. In a prayer meeting, this guy in a wheelchair did an impersonation of the lame guy from Scripture who picks up his mat and walks, and apparently he smashed it! (The impersonation that is, not the wheelchair.)

News travelled fast and what started as a weekly church prayer meeting ended up being known as "an outpouring".

Sometimes I hear stories of people being healed and I don't know about you, but sometimes I can be sceptical. Like when you hear that someone's leg has grown back, you think, *how does that work?* Then other times everything can be labelled as a "miracle", like if someone's smaller right earlobe has grown to be the same size as the bigger left earlobe. Forgive me for being facetious here (I'm probably just jealous because I don't have earlobes).

But going back to the point, for a known disabled guy in a wheelchair to get up and walk, surely that's got God's handiwork written all over it… hasn't it? And so it begs the question, does God heal today?

This line of thought will probably be too edgy for some and too safe for others, but I believe the answer is yes; yes God does still heal today. Not only that, but He involves us in the process. Romans 8:11 tells us that same Spirit that raised Christ from the dead lives in us. And by the Holy Spirit, who is deposited to us when we believe in Jesus (Ephesians 1:13), we have the power to do even mightier works than Jesus did (John 14:12), because it's not us, it's God in us.

Matthew 17:20 tells us that having faith shifts Kilimanjaros, that when we speak it out and believe it, mountains can pack up their things, hire a Transit van, and move (it would have to be one of those long-wheelbase vans with a high roof, I mean they are mountains after all). But here's the question – was this verse meant to be taken literally, or is it a hyperbole to simply make a point?

My theology hasn't changed dramatically over the years but I have been challenged to be more open to God showing up, because He can.

Maybe we do God a disservice by not engaging in a plea for Him to intervene and do what should be physically impossible (by the way, I'm lecturing to myself here).

The flip side of the coin, however, is that we have a responsibility, to God and people, to walk this line with humility and faith in equal measure. Holding such an emphasis on healing can be a slippery surface. Especially with new Christians or those on the fringes of faith. What if there's little foundation or a lack of understanding on the bigger picture of the Gospel? What happens when God doesn't heal? What happens then? Do we inadvertently make God out to be a liar to those seeking Him? Is He no longer trustworthy?

And what about those passages in the Bible that reference trials and suffering with a "when" rather than an "if", that speak about brokenness and sucky things as part of the furniture because it's a result of living in a broken world? And so again we seem to find this contradiction. That to follow Jesus we have the power, through the Spirit, to bring about the impossible, alongside the knowledge that if we walk in the footsteps of Jesus, suffering is not just a probability, it's a dead cert.

If you've lost my train of thought, allow me to pause the tangent and sum up thus far.

- I believe God healed (past tense).

- I believe God heals today and uses the church empowered by the Spirit (present tense).

- I also believe God will continue to heal (you've guessed it... future tense).

But in my mind, we haven't reached the heart of the issue here. We haven't quite excavated the real bone of contention. If God heals,

Why does He heal some and not others?

And so we find ourselves in the same scenario as a conservatory in a safari park, we've got ourselves an elephant in the room and this "why" question is Dumbo.* I'm not writing this with clear-cut answers, I'm still on a journey with this stuff and the truth is you could find many other books or blogs from authors with way more experience and a better biblical understanding than yours truly.

But speaking humbly, after Dad passed, this became something I saw in a new light. It went from a soft-focus hypothetical to a crystal-clear image of reality. You see this is not just a question for the university debating team, it's not just an assignment on a theology course, and it shouldn't be about charismatic Christians getting one up on the conservative Christians because they've got their theology wrong, or vice versa.

This is not an argument to be won here; it's bigger than that because this involves real people, with real lives in real situations. This is about real people experiencing real triumphs and/or real tragedies.

Dad asked for prayer...

Over the years I used to pray with Dad that God would heal him. For a lot of his life he was in severe pain and had what seemed to be a sweet shop of tablets to take the edge off. I used to pray with Dad, for Dad. Sometimes I'd offer, occasionally he would ask, but along with the physical pain was the turmoil of what was rolling around in his head – he was diagnosed with depression and PTSD. Looking back, I was probably overly cautious with the way that I prayed. Sometimes I was so focused on trying to be biblically accurate with it being His will not ours, that I forgot to have the faith bit that God could actually do something.

But when we prayed, there were more God moments. I wanted Dad to know that whatever was bothering him, he could always turn to God with it. I wanted him to know that even though the answer might not be what we're looking for, we're always egged on to ask the question. And when we did pray, what would happen more often than not would be that a peace came over Dad. Maybe his vertebrae didn't realign in his back but he did experience calmness, gentleness, and peace. And knowing just a portion of what he battled with, I think that's epic.

(And reversing the issue, as I mentioned in "Healing Moments", God has most definitely been doing a healing work in me with my grief.)

End of the road?

In the end Dad wasn't healed (though you've probably picked up on that if you've read up until now). And another truth is, after the consultant told me the news that it was the pancreatic C word, after she told me we were looking at days as opposed to weeks or months, after that – I don't think I prayed that God would heal Dad physically. Instead I wept, but with a profound determination to make every morsel of time we had left together count. I wanted him to feel safe, to feel loved, and to know he was not alone. And with that was an undeniable hunger to see Dad healed, not physically, but spiritually.

When we address the issue of healing and the mystery that can often surround it, we recognize that a big part of doing faith with God is that life can sometimes be a bit of a mystery.

In the well-used wedding passage of 1 Corinthians 13, Paul reminds us that we know and prophesy in part. But we're not left hanging, are we? Because along with that part of the passage also comes the hope bit, that when the perfect arrives the knowing and prophesying "in part" stuff leaves for good. And this is not a concept or a picture, this Perfect has a name, and that name is Jesus.

You see I think there's a greater narrative going on here and Isaiah covers it in his prophecy of Jesus.

> *"But he was pierced for our transgressions; he was crushed for our iniquities; upon him was the chastisement that brought us peace, and with his wounds we are healed."*
>
> Isaiah 53:5

We are a part of a great paradox that is the "now and not yet" kingdom of God.

He offers us to join Him in the healing process that He will ultimately finish. And that's just it – He will finish it to the point that it's completely completed. If we count on God, if we put our trust in Him, if we bank on Him and put our chips on Him – He will heal us.

The truth is, I don't really know why some suffer and others don't, why some are miraculously healed here on earth and others aren't. I don't have the checkmate answer. But I do know that when we don't know, we get to put our trust in a God that ultimately does. We get to put our trust in a God who will heal a broken world in all its fullness.

DAI DICTIONARY

Dumbo – clumsy elephant with the big ears (and probably earlobes too).

PRAYER

God
I ask humbly
If You would heal me.
Heal me when I hyperventilate
Heal me when I get in a panicked state

God
I say confidently
Thank You for how You've already healed me.
For the times Your grace has gifted me
For the moments Your mercy has lifted me
I ask humbly
That you continue Your holy healing in me.

God
Thank You that You pick me
to be part of Your kingdom-bringing project

Help us to have mountain-moving faith in You
In healing or hurting
Help us to always turn to You
Even when we feel like some prayers don't get through,
to You

Dad didn't beat that life-sapping cancer
But help me trust in You, even when I don't have the
answer.

For those who need Your healing hands
May they know Your peace in all Your plans
May we all know Your peace
As You reveal to us Your
   life-giving
      love-bringing
         hope-filling
and
   tear-ending
      plans.

RE: PRAYER

Yes.
I do have plans
That you know My love for you is one of those plans
I'm
with you
and
for you
I hope that this lands.

Yes.
I am healer.
My Son showed you it's part of My plans
My Son revealed My healing hands.

Pray to heal
Pray to move mountains
You're bringing My kingdom,
On that – I'm counting.

And when you search through My Scripture
May you also find My bigger picture.

You see healing is now but it's also in part
My plan's restoration
Like Eden
at the start.

I hate it when you hurt.
And I hate cancer
But please keep trusting Me
even when you don't have the answer.

May you come to Me with all your fears
And know one day I'll wipe away your tears.

"He will wipe away every tear from their eyes, and death shall be no more, neither shall there be mourning, nor crying, nor pain anymore, for the former things have passed away."

Revelation 21:4

This season has taught me the importance of the posture of

Receiving over Ritual

Devotion over Duty

+

Surrender over Striving

Chapter
13

GRIEF IS NOT EXCLUSIVE TO THE GRIEVERS

As I've journeyed through grief I have been really aware that those who walk beside grievers go through their own grieving process. I won't pretend it's always been straightforward for me and Cath. There have been times where it's been tough to "get" each other because she's never suffered a loss like I have, but the flip side is, I haven't had to walk beside and support someone through their grief, as she has with me.

In this chapter, I've asked Cath to share some of her thoughts and experiences on this journey. I've asked her to share ways in which she has grieved too. I like to think I'm pretty self-aware but I know I need Cath to point out my blind spots and I'd love her to share about my story in a way that I never could. My hope is that this book will help put into words what it's like to suffer loss so "the grief going through-ers" know they are not alone.

It's also for the "grief bystanders", or those who haven't grieved, in the hope that they may better understand what it might be like. That said, it's important to acknowledge that we who grieve need the wisdom of "the grief standing by-ers", those who are holding our hands every step of the way.

Over to my "grief standing by-er",

Over to my bestest friend and my most favourite wife.

Over to the beautiful short blonde Welsh one with a cheeky laugh and a big voice.

Over to the cute one.

(Also, just a heads-up – if she refers to some guy called "Dafs", don't panic, that's just me.)

"We can ignore even pleasure. But pain insists upon being attended to. God whispers to us in our pleasures, speaks in our conscience but shouts in our pains; it is His megaphone to rouse a deaf world."

(C. S. Lewis, *The Problem of Pain*)

Walking this journey of grief with my best friend and main man these past three years has presented a new sort of megaphone in our marital journey. I will never forget the moments down in Glangwili hospital that cloudy Monday afternoon. The reverberating words in slow motion, namely "Pancreatic cancer" and "He possibly only has days left", seem to have buried themselves deep in my core. I watched "my" Dafs confronted with the loudest megaphone of pain that awoke a season of some of the most tragic, tumultuous, yet cathartic and ironically beautiful moments in our eight-year pilgrimage as the Woolridge household thus far.

Four-letter words have played a big part in our partnership; here are some to name a few...

LOVE – learning the high roads and valleys of what makes this word beat. I never knew that it would offer such heights and depths of beauty and frustration.

LIFE – learning to live life in all its fullness and what that meant not just for "me" any more, but in partnership with this new three-stranded cord needing such delicate attention.

WIFE – I was learning the rhythms of being one half of a whole... seeing so much selfishness in me that I had never seen before, yet also having someone to point out my blind spots and beautiful parts in the most liberating of ways.

CHOC – not gonna end this word, as it can be followed by oholic, monster, addict... Choc plays a big part in our Wooly cupboards. And just to clarify, I'm a Cadbury girl, he's a Galaxy player!

These are just a few four-letter words that have played starring roles in our journey together. Yet on that February day there was a four-letter word that seemed to storm into the room, megaphone at volume capacity, and take centre stage, screaming its way into our lives. A four-letter word that has echoed amidst the walls of our marriage ever since in a new way to how we knew it before... the four letters that spell out PAIN.

At first I didn't know how to deal with seeing my other half experience such a level of this four-letter-worded curveball. In some ways I felt so oblivious to the extent of it, having not grieved before, yet in other ways I had this growing knowledge of my own pain in response to seeing my Dafs lose what was such a big part of him.

Much of those first weeks, even months, seemed to

be a fog of confusion. I felt as if I was in a soul tug of war between knowing I needed to be there like never before for my beloved husband who was going through the toughest moments of his life – and then this weird sort of pain that made me feel selfish most of the time. It was rooted in an ironic sort of grief at seeing Dafs hurt so deeply, and yet also, again selfishly, in not having my Dafs as the rock he had always been to me in our marriage so far. I was almost grieving to have my husband back!

This weird sense of my own kind of loss mixed with the confusion of not understanding some of Dafs' new reactions in the irregular emotions that grief brings, often made me feel so misunderstood, isolated, lonely, and sometimes angry. In some first instances I reacted totally wrongly and would talk to Dafs about "my" pain.

Guilt has played a big part in my deep soul as I've walked alongside Dafs and had to battle with selfishness bigger than I knew was possible to live inside me.

But what I realized as I spent more time in this garden of grief is that I needed to learn patience to a new level, to accept that I would not always understand, and with God's help to learn new rhythms of love. 1 Corinthians 13 rhythms: persevering love, a love that trusts, and a love that always hopes. This love doesn't come from striving, but from surrender. A love that first loved me so I could receive it, and then in the knowledge of it, be able to give it away. This love rooted in Emmanuel taught me, in those selfish, guilt-ridden moments, to grab a hold of the love of our heavenly Father. He held out to me a grace that was greater than the sum of my selfish sin, a mercy that knew my good-for-nothing state during difficult days where I didn't understand Dafs, and a love that showed me tenderness which I had done nothing to deserve but received anyway.

This season has taught me the importance of the posture of receiving over ritual, devotion over duty, and surrender over striving.

Peace

Learning these new routes of peace became an adventure, to say the least. I like being in control. I like fixing people. I like solutions. But in this season... there was no quick fix-it solution, there was no way of controlling emotions or knowing what a day might bring. It was all about submitting my precious husband and his four-letter battle, plus my confused grief, to a God who is far greater than it all.

For the first time there were no obvious signposts. Every morning I would ask the Prince of Peace to come and sit amongst us, whatever wave of grief seemed to batter my Dafs on this "today". Part of this process was learning the beauty of exchange – me giving God my despair in exchange for His peace. The only way I could receive this peace was by giving up the right to understand what was going on in my precious husband's heart. For the first time I had revelation about what "peace that passes understanding" truly meant in its living, breathing form.

This peace taught me that I needed to give Dafs room. That meant not bombarding him with words and affection, not trying too hard, or always asking "Are you OK?", but instead trying to function in "peace" with Dafs – giving him the wide open space to breathe in each new step of this unknown grief journey without trying to navigate him through it. This was HIS grief and I was learning that I needed to be a shoulder and not a satnav! I was meant to support and not to signpost; the quicker I learned that the better.

As time passed I learned that in order to maintain the

sort of peace that aided Dafs' journey it was also important for me to acknowledge the pain that had become my story in this grief. I learned that this was something I needed to do outside of the boundaries of my marriage. So I journaled a lot of my thoughts and feelings as well as speaking to a close friend about this path less travelled. For a long while in the first months of Dafs' dad's passing I thought it too selfish to fully acknowledge my "grief". But as time passed I recognized that I was running from wounds that I needed to acknowledge in order to get them dealt with.

I was learning that being honest with a small group of people about how I was doing in this was really helpful. It was also really helpful to spend time trying to be honest with myself. I found that what I often did was ask Dafs how he was doing, and I almost dreaded his response. I felt deeply the lack of control in not being able to be the problem solver for emotions and a situation that I couldn't make better! But I learned that each morning the best thing to do before I even muttered a word to Dafs was to check in on myself, connect with my heart, and ask, "Heart, how are you today?" Often in this season it responded with "confused", "overwhelmed", "frustrated", but I learned more about the grace extended to me in whatever scenario my heart found itself in that day. Understanding where I was at helped me to better support my Dafs. Grace has helped me acknowledge that grief is a process and there is no expiry date. This journey of my amazing Dafs losing one of the centre pieces to his life jigsaw will always be a part of our story. There is no end date. This is now us.

What I have learned in these moments of the four-lettered megaphone stampeding through some of our days is that this word, "pain", is not an enemy. In many ways it is inevitable in our broken humanity... What I have also learned is that "unhealed pain" can become our greatest enemy if our hearts don't confront the collision.

I am so proud of my hero of a husband for every day not being scared to confront this symphony of pain that has often deafened everything else into insignificance. For those of us who walk oblivious in many ways to the path of grief, yet in some ways so alive to its shadow in the face of our most precious person suffering its grip, we too need to embrace the pain. Run towards it and not from it. Face the giant head-on, as scary and lonely as it often feels.

I have seen my Dafs throw his arms around this monster named Grief, and all the intense hardships that come in its wake, and commit to feeling everything, as heavy as that often seems. He has allowed himself to feel the anger, the hurt, the grief, the frustration, the regret, the loss steamroller over his soul on a daily basis to different degrees. Yet inside the fire I have seen the other half to our whole learn and grow. Through observing my David, man after God's own heart, I have seen the fire of grief consume him yet liberate him in new ways... and I know this fire has equipped him to face future flames. In light of this I have invited the refining nature of this extravagant heat to consume my heart.

I have seen beauty in the brokenness like no other beauty I have experienced... I have seen it in Dafs and known it in me. This loss has left us both with a limp but somehow it's a beautiful limp.

PRAYER

(By Cath)

Lord Jesus
Thank You that it is You yourself who goes before us in
this time
– Abba, Almighty God, Emmanuel –
God with us, God surrounding us, in every moment.

May Your joy be our strength
And Your promises our confidence
Your schedule be our timing in every step of this
journey
And may Your unfailing love be our comfort in its
unwavering current.

Thank You that You do not give as the world gives
but You have left peace for us in every day that we will
walk through.
Peace is ours in Jesus.

You are the Prince of peace, the Prince of wholeness
and we dedicate every inch of this journey through grief
into Your hands.

"Peace I leave with you; my peace I give you. I do not give to you as the world gives. Do not let your hearts be troubled and do not be afraid."

John 14:27 (NIV)

I'M THANKFUL FOR THE REMINISCING FOR THE TEAR-FILLED GIGGLES AS I CHOKE UP AND CHUCKLE IN QUICK SUCCESSION

Chapter
14

A BEAUTIFUL BROKENNESS

Ever since I had the conviction to write this book, I knew there were key ingredients I wanted to add in. One was to be **real**. Not that I'm suggesting for a second that other books out there tackling the grief journey aren't, I just knew the only way I could approach this was by showing you my grief-stricken battle scars and for me to view my vulnerability as a strength and not a weakness. It never was going to be a book of observations written at a distance with some half-baked clichés. This was me sharing me – not just the bits where I come out smelling of roses, but the ugly bits too (where I come off smelling more like the stuff that fertilizes the roses).

And with the ingredient of authenticity kneaded through the batch, my hope was to bring out the flavour of **hope**. But it's not easy to arrive at hope straight off the bat, is it?

There's a great message in Pixar's* Inside Out* movie that picks up on just this. There's this relationship between two personified emotions of a little girl, called "Joy" and "Sadness". Joy is the person everyone wants to be around, she's the life and soul of the party, happy-go-lucky, and always positive. She's the kind of emotion you'd want to grab a coffee or do a road trip with. Then you've got Sadness. She's not the most fun person to be around, her coffee flask is always "half empty" rather than "half full". If Sadness called you up on a bank holiday, you'd probably let it go to voicemail. Joy tries to keep Sadness out of the way so she doesn't depress everyone. Joy wants to remember the good times and her positivity is pushed to the limit when she gets frustrated with Sadness for always wallowing in the tough times. It's only later on in the movie that we discover joy and sadness are completely connected. Joy realizes that the girl's best memory of experiencing joy only came after the girl came through the lowest moment of experiencing sadness. Does that make sense, or have I totally lost you and conjured up in you the emotion of confusion? (If the latter, check the film out!)

For me, it's similar here. How do you get to the other side of a tunnel? By going through it. True hope comes after you open yourself up to the journey; hope comes when you're prepared to trust it's there, even when there's a time that you can't see it straight in front of you.

Replaying scenes in my head

Looking back, of course I have regrets. If I had the chance to play out some scenes with Dad again I'd definitely do some things differently. One would be that I wish I'd spent more time with Dad.

There were days when he was alone in his flat with music blasting, just stuck in his own head. I think that if he was here now, I would get down that M4 quicker than Lee Mack gets round a punchline. I'd grab us a beer and just hang out with him. I wish I'd watched Six Nations rugby games with him. I wish I'd sent him fewer belated birthday cards and I wish the Father's Day messages had been more thought out and heartfelt.

There was one moment that for a while was a big stumbling block for me. It was a memory that really needed teasing out in my grief counselling. For Christmas 2012 Cath and I booked a holiday cottage in the Brecon Beacons. It was amazing. We had planned "me and Cath" moments, fellowship with family, and great mate moments. We spent most of the Christmas holiday in the heart of the Welsh countryside and enjoyed the festive season.

In the weeks coming up to the cottage visit, I knew I wanted to do something special for my old man. Usually around Christmas we'd spend a couple of hours swapping gifts and chats and then we'd go our separate ways... us to Cath's parents' and Dad to his girlfriend Tracey's. But this was going to be different (especially as Tracey had tragically passed earlier in the year). I didn't want this to be a dip in and out Christmas, I wanted to treat Dad. I wanted to cook him a mean roast dinner. I wanted him to kip over at the cottage and for me to just wait on him hand and foot. I remember giving the hard sell to Dad over the phone. At first he was hesitant. It was about an hour away by car.

"I just don't know if my back can handle the drive, Dave."

Dad had serious back issues from his time in the army and due to his PTSD he wasn't overly ecstatic about unfamiliar places either. Still, I wasn't taking no for an answer. I came up with as many solutions as I could find and he came round to the idea. *Yes. Result*, I'm thinking, as I typed "Dad coming over" into my phone calendar for "Boxing Day".

Then a few days before, Dad told me the bad news that he couldn't make it, he just wasn't up to it. My first reaction? I was gutted.

What I didn't realize back then now stares me in the face as if I'm playing a "first to blink loses" game. The blatant reality was that Dad only had six weeks left.

Six weeks.

No wonder he didn't feel "up to it". He was getting an absolute kicking by cancer and no one knew it. It was as if his body was in the ring with a UFC wrestler on steroids, while I was frustrated that I couldn't feed him up on Yorkshire puddings.

This conjures up in me an array of emotions, but one stands out among the rest: anger. Angry that we lost Dad too soon, angry with Dad for not coming to Brecon that Christmas, angry with myself for being so selfish wanting him there, angry with myself for not fully appreciating how unwell he was. Angry with myself for not doing more treats for him sooner.

When all is said and done, I wish I'd made more memories with my old man. I wish we all had.

Not all mouth, trousers too

Do I have regrets? Yes.

But Jesus didn't pay everything so I would carry on walking in guilt and shame. He came to make a glorious transaction – He took on my baggage, my guilt, my shame – He took it all for me and in exchange He gave, and gives, me freedom.

Some of my regrets are justified, but when I give them to God and seek His forgiveness, it's dealt with. Sometimes we try and reverse the transaction. You know, take the baggage back from the cross so we can carry the load and somehow find "peace" in our self-inflicted punishment. No chance this is right or godly. In fact I think it's got the stench of the evil one written all over it.

Jesus, on a cross, took the weight of sin on His own shoulders and in John 19:30 He said three words:

"IT. IS. FINISHED."

He wasn't being coy or a tease, there wasn't a small print that came afterwards, He didn't declare the good news and follow it up with a double-speed disclaimer to make sure He won't get sued for being misleading. Those three words from Jesus weren't said in an annoyingly catchy radio jingle, they were legit, they'd hold up and then some, these three words were full-on ironclad.

It.is.finished.

When He said those three words He meant it and when He rose three days later He proved He wasn't full of it. He wasn't a guy with good intentions and empty promises. He put death away, defeated it, beat it, smashed through it, and came out the other side of it… victorious. Capital "V", capital "ICTORIOUS".

Jesus rose again.

He spoke three words and proved them three days later.

His resurrection shows He had the authority to make such claims – He wasn't a prophet or just a good guy, He didn't do sleight-of-hand tricks and pass them off as miracles. Colossians 1 paints us a glorious picture of Jesus, and these truth-filled brushstrokes remind us that Jesus was and is God's Son, vis-à-vis, *ipso facto* – He wasn't all mouth, He was in fact holy trousers too.

So in light of this fact, when we take our mess and mistakes to God, when we take our rubbish and regrets to Him – may we know that it's dealt with.

Red herring regrets

The truth is that sometimes we want to revisit regrets and past failures and roll around in them. Sometimes we want to re-shackle ourselves when we've already been set free. When we do this, we need to take a detour and visit Jesus instead. He's our key to freedom and He can take the shackles off us – after all, He already carries them for us.

Other times we beat ourselves up when there are no grounds for it in the first place. In those moments we call out the fake allegations and like Babe Ruth from a New York Yankees baseball match, we *batter up* and knock those curveballs right out of the park. (Cue home run jingle.)

Tear-filled giggles and Meatloaf on repeat

As I reflect on writing this book, I know that this has been a really tough project. I've entered what were almost uncharted memories, places I'd discovered that I'd previously forgotten.

I've revisited memories.
The tough ones and the fun ones,
before and during those dire days.

I reflect on how far I've come in these last three and a half years.
I am grateful for my refined sense of perspective on life.
I'm thankful for knowing grief so deep, because I get to know how it feels to start coming out the other side.
I reflect on how God has kept me, even in the rough and the tough times.

I'm thankful for a profound yet painful snapshot into the heart of God. How the Father must've grieved in losing His Son, or how the Son suffered as He gave Himself up. Holy Trinity went through a temporary separation but did it so we could choose to be together, with Him.

I remember the meltdowns
The panic attacks
The semi-feeling of being in a dreamlike state as my inner monologue read,
"This can't really be happening, can it?"

I remember the prayers, the texts, and the tears.

I'm thankful for the reminiscing.
For the tear-filled giggles as I choke up and chuckle in quick succession.
Hitting the replay button on YouTube for Meatloaf* playlists.
Moments quoting Blackadder lines whilst remembering the grin that used to be on Dad's face.

This book has not just been a book on grief, it's been a celebration of a man who continues to amuse and amaze me.
This book has also been another big healing moment for me.
And if you're reading this, feeling paralysed by pain, my heart is that this book may have been a healing moment for you.
Even if it's for a micro-moment.
Even just a little.

If you've never been through the depths of grief, may this
book bring a blurry picture into a sharper focus.
Even if it's a pixel.
Even just a little.

For me, grief is a word with a limp.
It's how particles must feel after they've been in the Large
Hadron Collider.*

For to grieve is to collide with loss
To grieve is to be broken
Yet strangely
Somehow,
To grieve is still
Beautiful.

DAI DICTIONARY

Pixar – pick up any good animation
without songs in it and the chances
are it's made by these guys.

Inside Out – zoom inside a young
girl's head and find four emotions
with their own personalities. I've
lost you? Alright, Google it.

Meatloaf – whatever you say about
this guy, you have to say he'll do
anything for love (well, apart from
"that").

Large Hadron Collider – that big
thingamajig in Geneva where
people in lab coats do those
science-y experiments.

PRAYER

God
Grief has made me broken
Yet somehow, whole
There's no getting round the fact that this has taken its
toll

Though I may confess
That my struggle is getting less
I'm thankful that I can turn to You
Because in You I always rest.

God You have plucked me from the miry clay,
You've shown me grief is a badge I can display.

And
God You have reshaped me in so many ways.

I was full on empty
But You fill me full
I was broken
    Yet You show me
        Broken
            is
                somehow
                    beautiful.

RE: PRAYER

Of course you can put your grief badge on display
Know I know your brokenness,
I've been with you every step of the way.

Though you may confess
That your struggle is getting less
I'm glad you know My promise
Yes
In Me you CAN rest.

I know the times when you battled to cope
But know I was with you
And still brought you hope.
But I'm not just past tense
I'm present too
I'm also future
And I want it with you.

Know that I'm here for you
    Every grief step
        Every stage
            Know the truth that you're not alone
For I will be with you until the end of the age.

"And behold, I am with you always, to the end of the age."

Matthew 28:20

TWITTER TRIBUTES

I asked people who were close to Dad to share their own tribute to him through the medium of the tweeting bird (140 characters or fewer).

Here they are…

> **@Jess…**
> I could say so much about u, but can't express it in words –instead, my work will do the talking for me, &I know u would've understood that.

> **@Mam…**
> U were a good, brave &principled man who always worked hard when u were well. Immensely proud of all your children &thought the world of them.

> **@AuntyMarian…**
> Thankful 4my protective loving brother, turned guardsman. Proud 2c u on your passing out parade. You faced ill health with fight & courage.

@UncleGraham...

Gerald was generous to a fault, if anybody was down on their luck he would always help and think about himself later.

@Cousin Juls...

Uncle Gerald sadly missed but never forgotten. Memories and stories of his life that will always make me smile. #Crazy #Funny #Generous

@CousinRuth...

My uncle was cool, funny and had such a kind heart. Loved his family, beamed with pride for his children. Reminded me of mum; so similar

@CousinSarah...

My Uncle was kind hearted & funny. Mr. Positive! I still laugh about your unrelenting insistence that your Honda Jazz was the best car ever!

@CousinEmz...

Generous to a fault. A signed Scarlets rugby ball was too much for fixing a laptop. But it always makes me smile and think of Gerald.

@Gar...

Kind, caring &gentle. U had time 4everyone. Your advice 2me as a part time biker was invaluable. U R sorely missed. Always my friend. Gary.

@Wyn...

Gerald. Happy that you crossed my path a west is best rock music loving Cymro, proud family man, friend and Welsh guardsman. #SeeYouSoon.

@TheMightyAl...

Straight talking with your wisdom.

You taught me lots Ger & I taught you how 2fish properly!

Miss you so much. Thank you 4enriching my life.

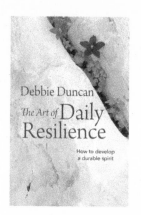

The Art of Daily Resilience

How to develop a durable spirit

What do you do when life gets tough? How do you pray when words fail?

Drawing upon personal tragedy, and her working life as a nurse teacher and a pastor's wife, Debbie Duncan shares her insight into what constitutes resilience: the ability to cope, to stay on course, to bounce back. She considers what is required for physical, mental and spiritual durability, interweaving biblical teaching with personal anecdote and sound advice.

Resilience is not innate; it's an ability to be acquired and fostered. It's an art. This book is an investment; a seed of faith that can be harvested when hard rains fall.

"This is not just a powerful story to touch the heart, it is a practical handbook to equip the mind and a window into the Heart of God to thrill and bless the spirit – a rich feast!"

JENNIFER REES LARCOMBE

ISBN 978 0 85721 781 3| e-ISBN 978 0 85721 782 0

Also from Monarch Books:

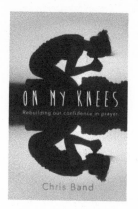

ON MY KNEES

Rebuilding our confidence in prayer

Life has a tendency to knock our confidence in prayer. In the face of persistent difficulties, our prayer-fuelled hopes can be overwhelmed by such despair that we end up "on our knees" – not so much in prayer, as in defeat.

In this honest and engaging book, Chris Band discusses the issues that we may have about prayer but were perhaps afraid to ask: Is prayer wasted effort? Is God less involved in the world than we might wish? Is his will going to be done anyway, whether or not we pray?

We discover that our prayers, far from being squandered by God, are powerfully and consistently used by him – both to build his relationship with us and to build his Kingdom through us.

This encouraging and practical book will inspire and lead each of us afresh, to be on our knees, in prayer.

"Biblically rich, and readably practical, this is a most helpful and encouraging companion on the journey of prayer."

REV DR CHRIS WRIGHT, LANGHAM PARTNERSHIP

ISBN 978 0 85721 775 2| e-ISBN 978 0 85721 776 9